Application of an Input-Output Framework

to a Community Economic System

Application

of an

Input-Output Framework

to a

Community Economic System

by

Floyd K. Harmston and Richard E. Lund

UNIVERSITY OF MISSOURI STUDIES VOLUME XLII
UNIVERSITY OF MISSOURI PRESS · COLUMBIA

To Winifred and Lillian

Foreword

IN RECENT YEARS considerable interest has developed concerning the functioning of economic systems of less than national extent but above the level of the individual producing and consuming units. This interest stems largely from a realization that regions and communities, while greatly influenced by national trends, deviate considerably at times from them.

This treatise deals with community systems. Communities differ from regions usually on the basis of geographic size. However, they also tend to have considerably more economic cohesiveness than do regions. Defining a community system is no easy task. It can be viewed as a cluster of activity, people, and producing units occupying a specific and recognizable geographic area, the members of which have a common interest.

The authors' interest in community systems developed through work done in the state of Wyoming. That state happens to be a rather ideal laboratory. The greater part of its population of about 340,000 lives in towns and cities scattered over an area of approximately 98,000 square miles. As a consequence, the state is divided into many fairly isolated community economic systems, twelve of which were studied quite intensively over a period of years, from 1950 to 1963.

Thus, the discussion here represents the results of experience plus some steps forward into hypothesized situations. In order to improve this framework as well as to make it more closely applicable to areas with less ideal laboratory conditions, we examined the methods reported by other regional and community researchers. Where they apply, we have incorporated other workers' ideas either as background or as techniques. It is hoped that this book will provide information to people who might avoid an interindustry approach because of the prevalent feeling that it requires a prohibitively large budget for data collection. Actually, many so-called economic base studies will result in the collection of as much information of a substantive nature as is needed for calculation of input-output. The choice often seems to be whether the information is collected and organized in a systematic framework or in a much less coordinated manner. The discipline imposed by an input-output table can help in the collection of data. Thus, less rather than more effort may be needed than for many less-disciplined approaches.

Another objective in planning this work was to counteract a fairly prevalent argument that, aside from some theoretical considerations, interindustry techniques are useful only in the analysis of large regions. That argument holds only if one is squeamish about using gross sales rather than margins for the wholesale and retail sectors. Actually, the use of a dollar-turnover approach has a great deal of value when one is considering local economies. We have used this technique quite successfully in the analysis of an economy with less than 15,000 inhabitants. In this instance we developed a 15 × 15 table. An even larger table could have been developed by further disaggregation of the retail sectors. The hypothetical community of Rawhide, used as an illustration in this treatise, has a table applicable to a community of about 20,000 persons.

It is true that larger tables result from studying larger and more integrated communities. This does not necessarily mean that the results are any more meaningful or any more interesting than those produced by the smaller tables. The interindustry approach furnishes an ideal theoretical framework for analyzing a community economic system of any size.

It should be emphasized at this point that the concept of input-output that is utilized in this book is not the usual one. In our approach the multipliers developed represent dollar turnover or money velocity. This means that a purchase by wholesale trade from local manufacturing is regarded as an input to the wholesale industry; purchases by retailing are regarded as inputs to the retail industry. In using this approach, it is recognized that the usual concept of a production function, which is the basis for most input-output analysis, does not apply. Dollar turnover is much more easily understood by those engaged in community development than the usual production multiplier; the data are much more easily developed; the roles played by tourist trade, transfer payments, and expenditures by the federal government are much more easily assessed; so long as the analyst understands what he is dealing with, the analysis is just as effective.

F.K.H.
R.E.L.

University of Missouri, Columbia
Iowa State University, Ames
July, 1966

Contents

CHAPTER I

Introduction

INTEREST IN THE SMALL LOCALIZED ECONOMY or community economic system has greatly increased in recent years. Much national legislation has aimed at helping communities that are in economic trouble, and millions of dollars are spent each year to promote orderly community growth and to prevent local economic decline. Yet, despite this interest, very little is known about the community economic system. Economists have in the past concentrated more often either on national units (macrosystems) or on the most elemental units (microsystems). Consequently, from a theoretical as well as from a practical standpoint, this is a new field of endeavor.

As will be explained later, community economic systems are the building blocks of macrosystems. It might therefore be expected that an increased understanding at the community level would do much toward improving insight into a macrosystem. It is here that rapid changes within the macrosystem are manifested and become most clearly evident. Seemingly, gradual changes in a large system are often the results of the averaging of much more spectacular changes in the smaller systems of which it is composed.

In turning to the more practical standpoint, current emphasis upon community development and industrial growth points up the need to understand the workings of community economics. Such understanding can help in giving guidance to development efforts and in pointing out types of industry that will bring maximum return to the local community. It will show indirect relationships that exist. As an example: Farmers do not ordinarily consider tourist trade to be important to them; an analysis can show the extent to which the farmer's dollar is dependent upon the tourist's dollar.

In the complicated, fast-moving world of today, local public administrators need to know the impact of impending changes before they occur. Businessmen are interested in the effect of such changes on their markets, particularly local markets. Labor officials should know not only what impact their own policies have on the welfare of their union members but also how certain changes in the industrial complex would affect them. State and national government officials should also be interested in communities. The success or failure of many national and state policies and activities is determined within the confines of community systems. It is there that the impact becomes most evident. For example: A decision to drop a particular type of weapon from production may not be of any great significance nationally, but in the community where it is manufactured the impact on all facets of life may be tremendous. Public officials are often startled by the reaction of local people to their decisions. If they better understood the workings of a community economic system, they would be in a better position to analyze decisions—and their effects—before they were made.

On an international basis, many newly emerging nations could be helped to understand and set up good economic policy if more were known about the way economies develop and operate. An understanding of the community economic system would also be of value in delineating the macrostructure within which local economies should operate. In a strictly agrarian world, perhaps this lack of understanding was not important. In a partially industrialized one, it was important, but not so recognized. In the space age, with the associated rapid rate of change, such understanding is critical.

In the sections to follow, special emphasis is given to developing some concepts concerning what a community economic system is and why it exists. Of special importance is the concept of an economic base. The problem of constancy in basic and nonbasic relationships is given attention from both a theoretical and an empirical basis. Upon this background a framework for analysis is constructed in Chapter III. Initial attention is given to possible measurement units and advantages and disadvantages of each. An input-output framework is then described and a working example provided. While not all possible frameworks of economic base analysis are examined, a few popular techniques are compared to the input-output framework proposed. Some progress into applying the input-output framework to any community economic system is made in Chapter IV, which concerns definitional problems and industry and sector delineations. In Chapter V problems of data collection are discussed. In Chapter VI, the many practical uses of the framework proposed are discussed in detail. Attention is turned to measuring the current economy, possible changes, and forecasting. The many places in which an input-output type analysis would fit in general purpose surveys are covered.

Throughout the book, an understanding of current economic thinking and of commonly used survey practices is assumed. Nevertheless, as neither the authors nor the readers are likely to be theoretical economists, background concepts are furnished as discussion proceeds.

Chapter II

Concepts

In initiating any study, a prime requirement is some concept of the problem to be examined. Particulars to be analyzed or tested are then extracted from that conceptual base. Consequently, a fairly rigorous development of the term *community economic system* will be the first topic for consideration.

Economic activity can be viewed as developing within a geographic framework for which natural resources, physical configuration, and the matrix of technological conditions are given.[1] Each geographical point within that framework is unique with respect to these influencing factors. Each such point is also isolated to some degree from all other points by the friction of physical distance or some other geographical factor. Microunits are introduced into this pattern. They consist of firms, people, and governmental units, who perform functions as producers and consumers. Generally speaking, each unit, acting as a producer, produces more of certain goods and/or services than it consumes. Acting as a consumer, it consumes more of certain other goods and services than it produces. The result is a system of exchange. While each microunit is somewhat unique with respect to consumption and production abilities, these abilities change over time. Further, each such unit is mobile and can move about in an effort to find the best situation to satisfy its insatiable desire for production-consumption. As these units move through time, within the constraints of the geographic frame, there is gravitation toward points where economic advantage exists. Greater specialization occurs among producers, resulting in increased production and the need for additional market outlets. Exchange systems become more elaborate and specialized.

As resources are exhausted and technological change occurs, there are further rearrangements. Clusters of activity decline and disappear; others grow and expand. New clusters spring up where there were none before. Elaborate trading systems develop, dominate the scene for a time, then fade away. Instability is in-herent in the system, and dynamics is a fact of life. Some forms of clustering and systematization remain, and at any particular time they can be identified. These geographic clusters of micro-units and their internal and external systems of exchange are of central interest in this treatise—the community economic sys-tems. That is, they are built upon massive trading with the world at large. Groups of these elemental systems can be aggregated into larger economies or extended systems of production and consumption. As such aggregation approaches a closed system —that is, one in which there is no trade with the outside world and all exchange takes place among units within the system itself—then a macroeconomic system comes into being. Such a large-scale aggregation usually has an element of political delineation and is often termed a national economy. However, national economies are not necessarily macrosystems, in the sense indicated above. The European Economic Community, for ex-ample, would be a macrosystem, but the individual countries would not.

Thus, it may be said that a community economic system is a primary cell within a macroeconomic system. Since a community economic system is a collection of microunits, it is certainly related to, but not the same as, the usual connotation of a micro-system. Because the community system has distinct characteristics when compared to either the micro- or macro-systems, it might better be defined as a *medioeconomic* system.

The fact that considerable economic interchange occurs within each cluster as well as between different clusters indicates that some degree of common economic interest is certain to occur within the cluster. As we move from the theoretical structure just submitted into the modern, complex, real situation, common economic interest becomes one key determinant in delineating a community economic system. This interest may be the result of employment in, and dependence upon, one or a few basic in-dustries. It may be due to the type of economic self-sufficiency that develops around a common shopping center. It may be due to geographical location or a spatial isolation. In short, it is tied to the economic advantage of the particular point.

For this treatise, a community economic system is defined as *a collection of activity, people, and producing units occupying a specific and recognizable geographic area, the members of which have common economic interests.* In making this definition it is not intended that the many social and political factors that enter into the development of a community are to be ignored. It is necessary to stress, however, that these other factors are usually expressed as some part of economic advantage when growth or decline of a community is analyzed.

The Concept of the Economic Base

The theoretical structure for the economic base concept has been developed in only a fragmentary manner. The authors do not presume to develop an all-encompassing framework here. Some discussion of theory appears necessary, however, for proper understanding of proposed analytical tools. Empirical information will be inserted at various points to relate theory to the real situation.

In previous discussion of the concept of a community economic system, it was established that the economic functions of production and consumption are carried on by microunits. These microunits are mobile, and, upon introduction into a heterogeneous geographical framework, they tend to cluster in places where the situation is such that it produces a comparative advantage of some sort. Each of these units is assumed to achieve a degree of specialization, in that it produces more of some goods or services than it consumes and consumes more of other goods and services than it produces. This specialization establishes the need for trading—both within the local cluster and with units in other clusters.

Interdependence between input and output for each microunit is assumed, since something cannot be produced from nothing. Inputs include raw materials and other factors of production— some of which are resources of the area—others are the output of other microunits in the cluster, and still others are imported from other clusters. In addition, we will assume for the economic base concept that input and output are not only interdependent but also that input must equal output for each microunit. No allowance is being made for accumulating or depleting inventories. (Savings will be allowed at a later point.) Of course, since input equals output for each microunit, then input would equal output for any community economic system. Since input must equal output, it can be assumed that an increase in output will require a proportional increase in input. The mixture and sources of supply of inputs do not necessarily remain constant, yet there are many factors that tend to hold the pattern constant in any given short-run period. These factors include such things as the desire of human beings to cling to familiar settings and the cost of making drastic changes.

In opposition to these "status quo" factors are the many forces acting to bring about changes in the input pattern by increasing the output. They include economies-of-scale in production and distribution, availability of resources, and many others. Of course, these factors, over time, even with constant output, contribute to a changing pattern of inputs.

An examination of real situations has shown that factors tending to hold input patterns constant predominate in the short run, while those conducive to change predominate in the long run. Empirical evidence will be submitted later.

On the basis of the above discussion, let us hypothesize that input patterns and sources of supply for any microunit are somewhat stable over time and for varying levels of output. This leads to an induction that the proportion of total input coming from inside the community economic system will remain constant over time, regardless of alternations in total input (or output), since the community economic system is nothing more than an aggregation of the individual microunits. Implied in this conclusion is a constant pattern of trade with the outside world. Total input for the system equals total output, since no allowance is made for building inventories in individual microunits and individual input was given as equaling individual output.

As an aggregate, units operating within the economic system are producing for two markets: one located outside the system (exports) and one located inside (local). An independent increase or decrease in the local market is not possible, since this market is determined by local input requirements that are hypothesized to be a constant proportion of total output. However, the export market (an exogenous factor) is not so restricted and can vary at will.

How does total economic activity or total output of the system vary with changes in exports? Converting the above argument into algebraic language will give an answer. It was hypothesized that:

$$X_i = Y_i$$

where $\qquad$ X_i = total input by the "ith" microunit
and $\qquad\qquad$ Y_i = total output by the "ith" microunit.
Also, a constant input pattern was assumed; that is, where $a_i X_i$ represents input to the ith microunit from the local system, a_i is constant for all values of X_i and, of course, of Y_i.

In aggregating these microunits into a community economic system we have:

$$\Sigma X_i = \Sigma Y_i$$

or $\qquad\qquad$ $X = Y$
where $\qquad\qquad$ X = total community input
and $\qquad\qquad$ Y = total community output.

Now, let A represent the total local input coefficient for the local system, that is:

$$A = \frac{\sum_i a_i x_i}{\sum_i x_i}$$

The coefficient A is constant here by reason of the assumption of a constant output relationship. Thus:

$$X - AX = \text{total nonlocal input.}$$

And since $\qquad\qquad$ $X = Y$,

$$Y - AY = \text{total exports.}$$

In denoting total local exports by Z, we have

$$Y - AY = Z$$

and the desired relation of exports to total output:

$$Y = (1 - A)^{-1} Z.$$

The factor $(1 - A)^{-1}$ is commonly called the community multiplier.

No mention has been made so far of a medium of exchange.

Assuming that one is in use and that there is mutual advantage in exchange, value of goods and services exported will equal value of goods and services imported. The value of total output is a function of the value of exports. Actually, economic activity can be measured in many units other than dollars. Other units of measurement equally appropriate for use in economic base analyses are discussed in the following section.

Viewing the community economic system in terms of the movement of dollars, it may be said that every community takes part in certain export activities that bring in "new" dollars from outside that community. Such export activities are often called basic activities, and the money they bring in is called basic income.

Upon being introduced into the community, these "new" dollars work their way through several hands before finally "leaking" out. In doing so, secondary activity or secondary income is produced. One dollar of "new" money thus produces more than one dollar of total economic activity or business. The community multiplier, when adapted to a dollar basis, quantifies this relationship.

For an example of the mechanical procedures involved, let us suppose that a tourist passing through a community purchases a meal from a local cafe for one dollar. Perhaps 30 cents will immediately leave the community to purchase additional food supplies; another 50 cents is paid in employee compensation; and 20 cents goes for utilities. Thus, on the first round 70 cents remains in the community. If the employee spends 40 cents at the local grocery but sends the other 10 cents out of the local economy to pay for a mail order purchase and if the utility company uses 10 cents to pay for its fuel supply (nonlocal) and pays the other 10 cents to its employees, at the end of the second round 50 cents remains in the community. It is easy to see that this sequence can go on indefinitely. But, to complete the example, suppose that the local grocery sends all of its 40 cents out to purchase new supplies and the utility company employee spends his 10 cents while on a vacation outside the community. This ends the sequence with no part of the original dollar remaining in the community. In adding up turnover it is seen that a total of $2.20 ($1.00 + $.70 + $.50 + $.00) in economic activity was produced by the original dollar. The multiplier here therefore amounts to 2.2. If such a tracing technique were used for all new dollars entering a community during a certain time period, a community multiplier could be obtained.

The community multiplier written earlier as $(1 — A)^{-1}$ has such sequence equivalence. Upon noting that A is always less than 1 (total imports cannot be reduced below zero level), mathematical theory provides that $(1 — A)^{-1} = 1 + A + A^2 + A^3 + \ldots$ In nonmathematical language, the original dollar is spent, the amount remaining is spent, the amount remaining from the amount remaining is spent, ad infinitum. Nevertheless, by reason of $A < 1$, the sum is always finite.

UNITS OF MEASUREMENT

A number of different units can be used to measure activity in an economy. They include such units as number of persons employed, personal income, value added, and gross sales.

Employment is used quite commonly for the determination of multipliers. Its greatest advantage is that the various state and federal labor programs make a great deal of information available. Also, several problems are faced in using employment as a measure. One problem is rapid automation or technological change, which alters the number of persons employed in relation to output. The forecaster must first forecast this change before using the multipliers in his forecast of economic activity. Other problems stem from the definition of "job." A half-time worker may be counted along with a full-time worker and/or those who work overtime. Still further problems stem from the fact that it is difficult to assign jobs to basic or secondary activities when an industry is engaged in both. In addition, with no change or even a decrease in employment, value of output can change considerably; the case of agriculture's decreasing employment and increasing output is a good example.

Personal income consists of wages and salaries, profits, dividends, property income, interest, government welfare and retirement payments, inheritances, and any other activity that brings money into a household. Once again its major strength as a measure lies in the availability of information. Further, it can be demonstrated that the relationship of wages and salaries to output is more nearly constant than is the relationship of number of workers to output. Its major weakness is that it treats only a limited part of economic activity, even though it is probably the most important single part.

Value added is the sales of a firm less the cost of materials purchased from other firms. Its major strength is that it avoids double counting, since the cost of materials purchased from other firms represents sales by those firms. For example, goods produced by a local manufacturer and sold to a local wholesaler have a certain value, X. The wholesaler then adds his margin to cover his services in making the commodity available in proper amounts and condition to retailers. Its value is now $X + W$. The retailer then adds an increment to cover his activities, and the value of the product becomes $X + W + R$.

In using gross sales as an indicator, the sales of the manufacturers would be recorded as X, sales of the wholesaler as $X + W$, and sales of the retailer as $X + W + R$. A simple sum of transactions in the economy would amount to $3X + 2W + R$. Thus, there is a triple counting of X and a double counting of W. The value-added approach avoids these repetitions.

A major drawback to value added is the difficulty involved in determining the amount in the first place, besides allocating that amount to factors defined as residing either within the model or without the model. Numerous decisions must be made regarding what is to be considered cost of materials, especially when services are concerned. When households and government are included in the model, a question also arises concerning the deduction of personal income taxes paid to state and local government. They might be considered payment for services rendered.

Gross sales consist of total transactions. Often a major drawback to their use is the tendency to double count, as explained previously. However, this drawback is of little concern when an input-output framework is used. Some major advantages include ting calculation, the fact that there are numerous secondary sources from which to draw, and the fact that totals lend a double-entry aspect to the table and aid discipline.

Other measures exist also and may be used in some analyses.

COMPARISON TO OTHER MULTIPLIERS

Economic literature in recent years has been filled with discussion of various types of multipliers. Most people are probably more familiar with the national-income-based domestic and foreign-trade multipliers. In many ways a community multiplier is similar to these; however, some differences must be mentioned.

The domestic multiplier largely pertains to the income impact of an incremental difference between national savings and investment. The foreign-trade multiplier represents somewhat of an extension on the domestic-multiplier concept in that it pertains to the income impact of surpluses (or deficits) in foreign trade. Both concepts measure impact by taking into account turnover of new dollars within the economy before their withdrawal from current activity in the form of savings, paying for imports, and other means. Readjustment aspects for reaching new levels of equilibrium are included in the theoretical aspects of both multipliers.

The community multiplier concept differs most sharply from that of the domestic and foreign-trade multipliers in the workings of readjustment mechanisms. A community economic system is considered so insignificant—as compared to the outside world—that anything happening within the community is thought to have no effect on the outside world. In consequence, an injection of basic income into a community increases total activitiy momentarily, but, as the new money works its way out of the community, total activity again returns to its former level. In contrast, according to domestic and foreign-trade multiplier concepts, impulses of new money either from a change in the savings-investment pattern or from foreign trade will work its way through the national economy and in doing so will cause the effectors (savings, investment, and foreign trade) to provide further impulses to the national economy.

That is, as presented here and as usually conceived, community economic system concepts exclude all savings and investment activity from the model even if carried out by residents of the community. The authors' experience shows that aspect to be reasonable at least for smaller-sized communities and especially for short time intervals. However, when such models are used for long-term projections, a component denoting the relationship between local investment and community output growth is added. All large-scale capital investment and much of the smaller-scale investments seem to come usually from non-residents. That is, communities may be said to grow from without, while the nation grows from within. Nevertheless, it must be recognized that local savings over the long run and consequential investment is a factor that influences growth. Usually this influence can be handled more easily from a practical standpoint by outside model manipulation; this will be discussed later.

Another major difference between a community multiplier and the other multipliers of interest is the community multiplier's comprehensiveness. All current economic activity is included, regardless of whether local governments, businesses, or people are involved. If a dollar measurement system is being used, "a dollar is a dollar" regardless of who transfers it. A local person is considered as merely another microunit. In contrast, theories in which the other multipliers are embedded treat people and their spending-saving habits as a special sector and assume most governmental activity to be controlled by non-model decisions. While the community multiplier concept is more aggregative, it must also be recognized as being less rigorous by its omission of these important influences and by its reliance on what in many instances may be called at best only casual relationships. This casualness results from the need for an assumption of a constant output pattern made previously. Again, outside model manipulation, to be discussed later, as well as stratification of the relationships through the input-output type of model, can overcome much of this casualness in practical applications.

Of course, many other differences between a community

multiplier and domestic and foreign-trade multipliers will be apparent as our discussion proceeds. Many of these differences will arise only as a result of specific applications and from the use of particular bases of activity measurement. The reader may wish to examine further discussion on this aspect, presented by Kang and Palmer.[2]

SOME EMPIRICAL EVALUATIONS

Discussion up to this point has concerned the development of the theoretical structure of the community economic system, the concept of the economic base, and a community multiplier. How do these concepts compare to the real world?

Personal income data by states support the concept that communities in the United States are specialized production centers that are highly dependent on trade with other communities. The U.S. Department of Commerce, in discussing regional activity, states:

> It is believed that these two broad features—commodity production on the one hand, and generally similar importance of distributive and service (including government) pursuits on the other—provide a significant view of the geographic economies of the United States. They depict these economies as highly interdependent, linked to each other by a complex network of commodity and service flows. Further, they support a general view of the United States as a single "national economy" comprised of complementary, inter-related regional economies rather than as a "weighted average" of separate regional economies having a high degree of independence and passing through individually distinct stages of economic structure.[3]

The high degree of interdependence, which the economic base concept indicates as coming through basic income linkages, is especially stressed in viewing total personal income by states. For every year in which an appreciable national change has occurred, the direction of change has been the same in all or a very large majority of the individual states. This evidence would also support the view that change within a community would result from a stimulus from without rather than from within.

Personal income data by states also provide some insight into the stability of the type of trading relationships involved. Stability in this aspect is especially significant to use of the input-output framework, to be developed in the next chapter, besides being indicative of the stability of the economic base concept.

Bearing significantly on this point, it is to be noted that the profound economic changes of the past quarter of a century—featuring a vast growth in real national output and shifts in its composition—*have had relatively little impact on geographic differences in the broad industrial source patterns of income.* In 1929, as well as in 1955, both specialized commodity production and distributive and service activities were of roughly similar importance throughout the country. This fact emerges from an analysis of Table IX which provides data on civilian earnings for 1929 correlative to those in Table IX for 1955. . . .

These features of regional income patterns in the United States—specialized commodity production and similar emphasis upon distribution and service—are attributable to numerous factors. Among them are the location and character of natural resources, mobility of labor and capital funds, common institutions and laws, and access to broader regional and national markets made possible by the absence of trade barriers and highly developed system of transportation and communication.[4]

Nevertheless, it must be recognized that in examining data for states, we are involving geographic units that are not entirely comparable to the earlier given definition of community economic systems. Consequently, it is important that geographic areas fitting that definition be examined.

Strong support for the practicality of the economic base concept in some aspects would be obtained if all communities of similar economic characteristics and size possessed the same community multiplier. Kang, in an examination[5] of twelve communities within the Great Plains, selected on the basis of their similarity, obtained the results presented in Table I for 1957. Multipliers based on employment varied nominally between 2.0 and 2.8. The conclusion was reached that a multiplier in the range of 2.3 and 2.5 could be expected in most communities having characteristics similar to the twelve communities selected.

How do community multipliers vary between communities of different sizes and of varying economic characteristics? A detailed answer here would provide considerable insight into the dy-

TABLE I

COMMUNITY MULTIPLIERS

FOR

TWELVE SIMILAR COMMUNITIES

County and State	City	Multiplier*
AVERAGE OF TWELVE		2.393
Pierce, North Dakota	Rugby	1.966
Cottle, Texas	Paducah	2.071
Toole, Montana	Shelby	2.111
Harmon, Oklahoma	Hollis	2.179
Bent, Colorado	Las Animas	2.288
Tripp, South Dakota	Winner	2.328
Keith, Nebraska	Ogallala	2.468
Phelps, Nebraska	Holdrege	2.525
Hardeman, Texas	Quanah	2.537
Union, New Mexico	Clayton	2.679
Norton, Kansas	Norton	2.709
Clay, Kansas	Clay Center	2.792

*Based on employment.

Source: Edgar Z. Palmer, ed., *The Community Economic Base and Multiplier* (University of Nebraska, 1958), 22.

namics of the situation. Table II shows multipliers for communities containing from 12 million residents down to only a few thousand. These multipliers, while all were based on employment data, were not computed by identical methods. In some cases the division between basic and secondary activity was made by field survey; for others, national per-capita bases were used.

Except for New York City, there does not seem to be a significant correlation between size of community and size of multiplier. This is borne out by studies conducted in Wyoming communities as well as by conclusions reached in other studies[6] that show that the community multiplier varies for many reasons other than mere population encompassed. Paramount is the particular make-up of the community, such as the size of the shopping centers, types of industries bringing in basic income, and

TABLE II
COMMUNITY MULTIPLIER
BY SIZE OF CITY

City	Year of Study	Population in Thousands	Multiplier*
Auburn, Washington	1953	6	1.8
Streator, Illinois	1939	17	1.9
Medford, Oregon	1952	20	1.8
Oshkosh, Wisconsin	1950	42	1.6
Albuquerque, New Mexico	1948	100	1.9
Madison, Wisconsin	1952	110	1.8
Brockton, Massachusetts	1946	120	1.8
Wichita, Kansas	1950	200	2.4
Cincinnati Metropolitan Area	1940	787	2.7
Washington, D. C.	1947	1,000	2.0
Detroit, Michigan	1940	2,337	2.1
State of New Jersey	1948	4,800	2.0
New York Metropolitan Area	1940	12,000	3.1

*Based on employment.

Source: Edward L. Ullman, "The Basic-Service Ratio and the Areal Support of Cities," address delivered before the Association of Pacific Coast Geographers, Santa Barbara, California, June 8, 1953. In Edgar Z. Palmer, ed., *The Community Economic Base and Multiplier*, 31.

degree of specialization of production facilities. For example, agriculturally oriented communities, because of the tendency of farmers to purchase at home and of the requirement of numerous small-scale service industries, usually possess higher community multipliers than communities oriented toward large-scale self-sufficient mines. Geographic location, natural barriers to trade, and willingness of local merchants to compete with nearby communities also influence the multiplier. Resident income and consumption patterns as well as historic growth and economic maturity of the community are factors.

From the above discussion, it would be expected that the multiplier for any particular community would vary over time. An increase in mere size may be accompanied by a larger community multiplier. That is, secondary activity would increase by a larger amount than basic activity. Economic maturity could also bring about a larger multiplier. However, these long-term structural changes were considered in setting up the theoretical framework and should not invalidate its practical application. In fact, such long-term changes could be viewed as an implied part of the general analytical framework and be allowed for in particular applications.

A recent study of southwestern Wyoming provides an especially penetrating look at the short-run dynamics of the economic base concept.[7] Southwestern Wyoming offered a rather unique situation for studying rapid change, since historically the community was relatively stable. Vast changes then occurred in its basic income-producing industries, and a new level of stability was again reached. Before the upset in 1954 the community was dependent on coal exports, railroad work, a fairly extensive livestock industry, and tourists. After the change, by 1959 the economy depended on oil and gas exploration and production, a new mineral (trona), and some manufacturing, as well as on livestock raising and tourists. Coal became much less important, and railroading seriously declined. In looking at value of exports for specific years before and after the change, an over-all increase of 37 per cent was noted. Similarly, total commercial activity increased 37 per cent, and total output (we point out, however, that "total output" as used here is admitted to be a rather nebulous measure, and its use as a descriptive device is not necessarily recommended) as measured by, in essence, gross receipts of all commercial firms, local government, household income, and value of produced products sold, increased by 23 per cent. In contrast, hired employment dropped 13 per cent, population declined 6 per cent, while personal income increased only 8.8 per cent. Retail sales increased 4 per cent, while service-type sales rose 40 per cent.

These data seem to support only one conclusion—a paradox has been confronted. However, in going behind some of the figures listed above (as was done in the study), one finds that the changes occurring in the community were actually supporting the economic base concept. But, the relationship between basic income and total economic activity was found to be not so simple as portrayed by the mere construction of a community multiplier. While the southwestern Wyoming study showed that

*"total economic activity in a local economy has a measurable re-
lationship to basic income to that economy,"*[8] it also showed that
that "measurable relationship" rose from the stable relationships
existing between specific industries within the economy and that
it was *not* a relationship phenomenon of the economy in the
aggregate. Of course, it may be contended that the simple community multiplier could not be expected to remain stable under
such dynamic changes. But, if it does not, of what practical value
is it? The community that is undergoing rapid change in the one
especially needing analysis.

The study of southwestern Wyoming also pointed out some
inconsistencies in using various units of measurement for measuring the community multiplier. Employment as an indicator was
shown to have shortcomings; a mere aggregate of dollars to represent "total output" was equally hazardous. Additional information on the short-run dynamics of the community multiplier are
provided by Thompson in a study[9] of Lincoln, Nebraska. Over
a three-year period, monthly hired employment data were divided
between "localized" and "nonlocalized." The data for this somewhat stable community showed a sufficiently high correlation
and a regression coefficient sufficiently near the expected value
of a community multiplier to support the economic base concept
and stability of the community multiplier in the short run.

In summary, all empirical data examined seem to validate the
existence of community economic systems and the economic base
concept. The community multiplier itself, however, can be seen
to be a merely casual relationship. It is granted that for communities selected by similar criteria, the multipliers would
probably be identical. In turning to communities of different sizes
and economic characteristics, many reasons could be found for
communities to have different-sized multipliers. Data in Table II
supported this reasoning. Long-run changes in the community
multiplier for a particular community would also be expected.
The study of Lincoln, Nebraska, showed the community multiplier to possess considerable stability in the short run. However,
as portrayed in the study of southwestern Wyoming, when a
community is faced with extremely dynamic changes over a short
period of time, the simple community multiplier has little value.

A somewhat more complex measurement framework, nevertheless, supported the economic base concept. In actuality, the individual relationships existing between industries within that economy remained reasonably stable, but the aggregate of these relationships, the community multiplier, broke down as the pattern of basic income changed.

These empirical examinations indicate that community analyses could be logically built upon the economic base concept. For many communities, that analysis could be centered on constructing a community multiplier and evaluating how it might change or did change over time. However, for some communities, especially those faced with rapid change, the measurement framework should be extended so that underlying industry-to-industry relationships can be reckoned with. Chapter III will develop an input-output type framework which has that advantage in particular besides having many other analytical advantages.

CHAPTER III

The Input-Output Model

Iₙ CHAPTER II, theoretical evidence to support the idea of a community economic system was given. It was then established that the activity of such a system can be measured and analyzed.

In this chapter, emphasis is placed upon the application of one method, which we consider to be often superior, in making such measurement and analysis. This is commonly called the input-output method. It will be noted that its application to community economic systems is somewhat different than the national analysis for which Leontief originally developed it. This difference is due largely to differences in the systems being analyzed, since the model outline itself is identical.

Again, to emphasize the peculiar composition of a community economic system: Its most important characteristic is its dependence upon outside sources for its energizing force. All activity in a modern society is based upon specialization. Without specialization the elaborate systems of production and exchange that we are so used to would not exist. These are trading systems, and they can be defined in many ways, ranging from mere exchange between individuals to international trade among nations. The community economic system is a trading system, involving two rather specific types of trade, that among units within the system and that between the system and other systems.

The community economic system can, then, be defined as a collection of units (people, activities, producers, etc.) occupying a specific and recognizable geographic area, the members of which have common economic interests. These common economic interests tend to draw the units into a community. It is not essentially different from an individual trading unit, in that it sells its products and services to the outside world and uses the income to buy goods and services from the outside world. However, there is one major distinction: The income received from the outside is not immediately paid out for imports, but circulates through the community from hand to hand, creating a local market for locally produced goods and services. Eventually it must leak out again to pay for imports. Meanwhile, other exports are being made, and a continuous flow of new income is maintained.

It was concluded in the last chapter that the total output of such a community has a measurable relationship to, or can be said to be a function of, exports to the outside world. By making two assumptions, it was concluded that this relationship was of the form:

$$\text{Total output} = (1 - A)^{-1} \text{ (Exports)}.$$

These assumptions were: (1) that each microunit (either a producing or consuming unit, that is, a mill, a household, a farm, a retail store) maintains a constant input pattern with regard to kinds of inputs and sources of supply as total output varies, and (2) that the product mix of the output traded to the outside world remains constant, despite increases or decreases in total amount traded. The A appearing in the formula above is a constant coefficient denoting the proportion of input that comes from the community itself. Its constancy derives from the assumptions made. The factor $(1 - A)^{-1}$ is often called a community multiplier. It was recognized previously that this multiplier can be estimated through the use of any of several different units. Some of them are employment, payroll and other personal income, market value, and value added. Any of these can be used to measure total output and exports. However, they are seldom used to estimate A by itself, but instead to estimate $(1 - A)^{-1}$.

Upon examining considerable empirical information it was determined that the community multiplier denotes only a casual relationship. Such a relationship is of value in community analysis where stability exists in the system or where adjustments can be added by "outside formal model" manipulation, such as altering the community multiplier for a growing community as population increases. It is of considerably less value where fairly extreme change can be expected in the system. Yet, it is usually the latter type of system that is most seriously in need of analysis. This is where the input-output model can make its greatest contribution. It provides a more detailed analytical framework than is provided by a community multiplier, hence is more adaptable to peculiar situations.

The major difference lies in the extent of aggregation. Whereas the ordinary multiplier results from an aggregation of all units, input-output model aggregation of microunits proceeds only to the point of combining those that possess similar input patterns and trading characteristics. Determination of classes must, of course, take into consideration objectives of the study and peculiarities of the community. The combinations are often called *industries*.

The result is the construction of a multidimensional model whose general form is identical to that of the community multiplier, but in which the data may be placed in rows and columns. Now, instead of appearing as single numbers, total output and total exports are handled as rows of elements in a table. Each element in the row denotes output (or export) of a particular industry. Similarly, instead of one A denoting an input coefficient for an entire community, a multidimensional A is constructed, in which each element is an input coefficient denoting the relationship between any two local industries. Actually, the input-output model can be thought of as a stratified form of the community multiplier. On the other hand, the community multiplier might be thought of as a one-dimensional input-output model.

It is obvious, at this point, that the input-output model has some distinct advantages over the community multiplier framework. One of the most important of these is relaxation of the requirement that the pattern of output traded to the outside world remain constant as total volume of trade changes.

When observing communities undergoing dynamic change, it becomes quite apparent that much of the change is the result of a shift in the pattern of exports. For example, a community may have been historically dependent upon coal production, agriculture, and incidental oil production. Suddenly a shift occurs; coal production drops off and oil production booms. Under that situation, a casual community multiplier may be of some, but often only incidental, value. In order to find out what is really going on, the analyst needs several multipliers showing community support received from each industry. Such multipliers would occur in a model of the form:

$$\text{Total output} = M_c Z_c + M_a Z_a + M_o Z_o$$

where
M = multiplier for a particular industry
Z = exports of that industry
c = coal, a = agriculture, o = oil.

In order to forecast the effect of change, estimates of exports of each of these industries can then be inserted into the model. The input-output model can readily produce multipliers for such a model. Actually, what it does is make it possible to handle change by aggregating units into industries in such a way that the rule of constancy holds for each of the industries, even though it does not hold for the whole community.

Input-output goes much further than producing industry multipliers, however. It also produces submultipliers that reveal relationships between industries. Suppose, for instance, that information is needed concerning the effect of the drastic shake-up on receipts of local government or on retail trade. These relationships are readily made available by this method. The additional information is furnished by reason of an added dimension in the input-output framework, by which it produces submodels of the form:

$$\text{Retail store sales} = M_{rc} Z_c + M_{ra} Z_a + M_{ro} Z_o$$
$$\text{Local government receipts} = M_{gc} Z_c + M_{ga} Z_a + M_{go} Z_o$$

where

M_{rc} is a multiplier connecting coal exports to retail store sales,

M_{ga} is a multiplier connecting agricultural exports to local government revenue,

Z_o represents exports of the oil industry, etc.

Later discussion and examples will illuminate these points.

DEFINITION OF THE MODEL

An industry can be defined as a grouping of microunits meeting certain similarity requirements in terms of input and trading characteristics that are established by objectives of the analysis.

For any industry, say the ith industry, total output (sales) over a particular time period equals the sum of its output going to each local industry plus the output going to markets outside the delineated community economic system. That is, if there are n delineated community industries,

(3.1) $Y_i = \sum_1^n y_{ij} + Z_i$, $i,j = 1,2,\ldots,n$

where, as defined similarly before,

Y_i = total output for ith industry

y_{ij} = output by ith industry going to jth industry (endogenous transactions).

and Z_i = output traded outside the community economic system (exogenous transactions).

In making the assumption of constant input coefficients, that is, that input from the ith industry to the jth industry is a linear homogeneous function of total output by the ith industry for all values of output to be confronted in usage of the model, we have:

(3.2) $a_{ij} = \dfrac{y_{ij}}{Y_j} = $ a constant value

and upon substitution into equation (3.1),

(3.3) $Y_i = \sum_1^n a_{ij} Y_j + Z_i$, $j = 1,2,\ldots,n.$

This relationship may also be written

(3.4) $Z_i = Y_i - \sum_1^n a_{ij} Y_j$

and in matrix notation this becomes

(3.5) $Z = Y - AY$

(3.6) $= [I - A]Y$

where $Z = \text{col } (y_1, y_2, \ldots, y_n)$

$Y = \text{col } (Y_1, Y_2, \ldots, Y_n)$

$A = [a_{ij}]_{n \times n}$

and I is an $n \times n$ identity matrix.

Upon assuming that $[I - A]$ has an inverse, a condition met in essentially all practical applications, we have:

(3.7) $Y = [I - A]^{-1} Z$

which is a form identical to the community multiplier framework except for change in dimensions. Here, however, each element in the inverse matrix $[I - A]^{-1}$ denotes the amount of output from the ith industry used both directly and indirectly per unit of output traded by the jth industry outside of the community system. In contrast, the one-dimensional $(1 - A)^{-1}$ community multiplier indicates the amount of output used from the entire community system for each unit of trading carried on outside that system.

Again, as in the community multiplier model, no measurement units have been specified. As will become clear later, the authors prefer units at least comparable to the usual connotation of dollars worth of sales. However, it must be noted that the model itself does not make this requirement. In fact, output for one industry may be measured in barrels of oil, another in current dollar receipts, and another in head of cattle traded. Nevertheless, the model does require all output (or sales) by the ith industry to be recorded in identical units. That is, sales of oil in barrels cannot be added to sales of oil in dollars for the oil-producing industry. The requirement for constant input coefficients is essentially a requirement for input of raw materials, supplies, power, and even workforce to vary in direct proportion to that industry's output.

An input-output model, in which all trading activity is essentially regarded as sales in dollars, simplifies model construction and promotes understanding. As will be noted in the discussion of measurement units in Chapter IV, many definitional problems are confronted in constructing a community multiplier by dividing employment into "basic" and "secondary" categories. For example: A business selling material to a local processor whose final product is exported might be classified as "basic," yet a retail store selling groceries to the workforce of that processor might be classified as "secondary." In turning to the input-output framework and basing economic activity measurements on selling for dollars, the whole problem is circumvented. The criterion is simply: Who bought it?

MODEL FORMAT

Attention will now be turned from the explicit definition of the input-output model to a format commonly used in quantifying an economy by such a model. First, suppose that a community economic system can be properly analyzed by dividing all activity into three industries. Equation (3.1) would then usually be written in the following format:

TABLE III
A SAMPLE TRANSACTIONS TABLE

		Purchases			Exports	Total Output
		Industry #1	Industry #2	Industry #3		
S						
A	Industry #1	y_{11}	y_{12}	y_{13}	z_1	Y_1
L						
E	Industry #2	y_{21}	y_{22}	y_{23}	z_2	Y_2
S	Industry #3	y_{31}	y_{32}	y_{33}	z_3	Y_3

The section of the table containing the y_{ij}'s denotes endogenous transactions or transactions occurring among members of the model. Specifically, each y_{ij} denotes a sale by the ith industry to the jth industry. Of course this can be turned around, in that y_{ij} denotes a purchase by the jth industry from the ith industry. In other words, in viewing the y_{ij}'s as columns, purchases are represented, while viewing them as rows, shows sales. Of course the z_i's section shows exports (exogenous transactions), and the Y_i's section indicates total output or total sales.

In constructing an input-output model it is often of value to add an import (or nonlocal input) row to the transactions table in order to show a complete picture of all transactions. Then, upon conforming to an earlier assumption—total inputs equal total output for each microunit, hence for the entire system—Table IV is produced. In this table, Σz represents total exports by all industries, and a like definition is given to ΣY_i and Σw_i. Of course it should be stressed that the import row is not a functional part of the model.

A next step in any analysis is construction of an input coefficient table. Earlier it was assumed that all input coefficients were constant. These are the a_{ij}'s said to be equal to y_{ij}/Y_j. An example here is Table V. While the only functional part of this table is that containing the a_{ij}'s, the other ratios are usually included for descriptive purposes.

TABLE IV
A SAMPLE TRANSACTIONS TABLE

	Purchases Industry #1	Industry #2	Industry #3	Exports	Total Output
S					
A					
L Industry #1	y_{11}	y_{12}	y_{13}	z_1	Y_1
E Industry #2	y_{21}	y_{22}	y_{23}	z_2	Y_2
S Industry #3	y_{31}	y_{32}	y_{33}	z_3	Y_3
Imports	w_1	w_2	w_3		Σw
Total Input (Output)	Y_1	Y_2	Y_3	Σz	$\Sigma Y + \Sigma w$ (or $\Sigma Y + \Sigma z$)

TABLE V
A SAMPLE INPUT COEFFICIENT TABLE

	Industry #1	Industry #2	Industry #3	Exports	Total Output
Industry #1	a_{11}	a_{12}	a_{13}	$z_1/\Sigma z$	$Y_1/(\Sigma Y + \Sigma w)$
Industry #2	a_{21}	a_{22}	a_{23}	$z_2/\Sigma z$	$Y_2/(\Sigma Y + \Sigma w)$
Industry #3	a_{31}	a_{32}	a_{33}	$z_3/\Sigma z$	$Y_3/(\Sigma Y + \Sigma w)$
Imports	w_1/Y_1	w_2/Y_2	w_3/Y_3		$\Sigma w/(\Sigma Y + \Sigma w)$
Total	1.00	1.00	1.00	1.00	1.00

The a_{ij} segment of Table V is then used in forming the inverse matrix $[I - A]^{-1}$. An example of this manipulation is not provided here. Actually, the operations involved are usually of an extent that an electronic computer is required. The nonmath-oriented reader may compare the process to tracing out the detailed effects of each different industry receiving $1.00 in basic income.

Table VI shows a common format for submitting the inverse matrix. Each element m_{ij} is a miniature multiplier denoting both the direct and indirect effect upon the industry heading the row by basic income received by the industry heading the column. Of course these multipliers can be combined in any number of ways to various groupings of industries. Merely summing the columns produces a multiplier denoting the output that results from one unit of export by the industry heading the column.

TABLE VI

A Sample Direct and Indirect Benefit Table

$[I\text{-}A]^{-1}$

	Industry #1	Industry #2	Industry #3
Industry #1	m_{11}	m_{12}	m_{13}
Industry #2	m_{21}	m_{22}	m_{23}
Industry #3	m_{31}	m_{32}	m_{33}
Total Multipliers	M_1	M_2	M_3

An Example

From the above illustration we may now move to a numerical example. The area to be studied is that well-known community of Rawhide, a fine, old place dating from the days when bison roamed the plains and rawhides were a major commodity of export. While the place may be mythical, the data are based on an actual community of approximately 20,000 persons.

The transactions table for Rawhide is given as Table VII. This community has an economic base consisting of agriculture, minerals, nonlocal government activity, manufacturing, farm product handlers, travelers, a small wholesale export trade, and miscellaneous payments to households by outside sources. These are shown in the outside world demand sector of the table.

The first eleven columns and rows constitute local economic activity or the endogenous segment of the table. This is the matrix y_{ij} shown in the previous section. It is the part of the table that will be manipulated to determine the effect of dollar turnover or the effect of dollars introduced in the form of basic income.

Columns to the right of the local activity, or endogenous segment, make up the basic income-producing, or exogenous segment, of the table. Transactions here have earlier been termed as exports from the economy. In the format discussion, this section was assumed to be collapsed into a column vector $(z_1, z_2, \ldots, z_n)$. However, additional detail is given here, as is usually the case in actual applications.

All rows below nos. 1-11 represent imports to the community system. These were given the symbol w_i in the prior format discussion.

Columns of the transactions table are grouped into three sectors: (1) commercial and producing, (2) local final demand, and (3) outside world demand. The commercial and producing sector is made up of all local transactions pertaining to producing, servicing, and marketing a product; such transactions would naturally fit into the endogenous segment. The outside world demand sector denotes selling outside of the local community and fits naturally into the exogenous segment.

Local final demand, made up of local government purchases, resident household consumption, and sales by local firms to local investment, is divided between exogenous and endogenous. As will be discussed later in detail, the input-output framework developed herein can only handle adequately *current activity* transactions. Sales to local investment certainly does not meet the *current activity* criterion, for the decisions to invest are not directly linked with levels of current output. Instead, the decision to invest in a new building or in extra machinery may be the result of several years of planning. Also included in this column are sales by local firms to bodies not considered part of

TABLE VII

MONETARY TRANSACTIONS
RAWHIDE COMMUNITY, U.S.A.

19 —

PURCHASES *

| | Endogenous Transactions — Commercial and Producing Sector | | | | | | | | | | | Exogenous | | | | |
| | | | | | | | | | | | | Local Final Demand Sec. | | Outside World Demand Sector | | | |
(Sales)	Agr. 1	Min. 2	Const. Contr. 3	Manuf. 4	Trans. & Util. 5	Farm Product Handlers 6	Other Whls. 7	Retailers 8	All Serv. 9	Local Govt. 10	Local Hshld. 11	Sales to Local Invest.	Nonlocal Govt.	Travelers	Other	TOTAL SALES
1. Agriculture	3,629	-0-	-0-	3,946	-0-	3,808	13	53	-0-	-0-	-0-	-100	1,534	-0-	19,228	32,111
2. Minerals	-0-	3,443	-0-	-0-	309	-0-	-0-	-0-	-0-	-0-	-0-		-0-	-0-	28,860	32,612
3. Construction Contractors	53	1,015	509	14	9	2	5	35	43	13	103	1,627	4,783	-0-	-0-	8,211
4. Manufacturers	492	-0-	67	-0-	8	11	18	1,387	12	8	310	-0-	-0-	-0-	7,651	9,914
5. Transportation & Utilities	1,316	48	89	814	312	40	243	579	731	143	852	-0-	88	-0-	-0-	5,255
6. Farm Product Handlers	2,414	-0-	-0-	-0-	-0-	-0-	-0-	-0-	-0-	-0-	-0-	-0-	-0-	-0-	4,475	6,889
7. Other Wholesalers	1,209	472	101	15	84	7	41	4,499	286	136	19,377	3,215	37	1,463	354	7,204
8. Retailers	2,031	334	191	71	-0-	-0-	138	234	649	208	4,906	-0-	41	357	-0-	27,877
9. All Service	1,527	342	89	46	121	151	43	808	274	60	507	-0-	2,203	-0-	-0-	8,790
10. Local Government	722	844	27	-0-	293	31	32	236	518	3,223	-0-	-0-	3,954	-0-	-0-	5,300
11. Local Household	9,449	6,631	1,943	976	1,488	486	505	3,690	3,430	-0-	-0-	-0-	-0-	-0-	4,053	40,335
Nonlocal Government	841	2,142	66	99	175	45	682	212	125	42	4,266					8,695
Factor Earnings to Nonresidents[1]	857	11,573	604	381	641	4	142	945	1,336	49	711					17,243
Capital Consumption	3,657	3,468	219	128	330	40	60	342	636	-0-	-0-					9,080
Imports	3,914	2,300	4,306	3,424	1,285	2,264	5,282	14,907	750	318	7,817					46,567
Other										1,100[2]	810[3] 3,284[4]					2,238
TOTAL INPUT	32,111	32,612	8,211	9,914	5,255	6,889	7,204	27,877	8,790	5,300	40,335	4,742	12,640	1,820	64,621	268,321

*In thousands of dollars.

[1] Net income for all corporations, any interest and rent paid to nonlocal persons plus all interest on capital (includes depletion for minerals).

[2] Revenue leaving to amortize new facilities instead of actual depreciation and savings (savings and investment).

[3] All house payments including interest.

[4] Savings, personal.

the local community, such as a local contractor for local highway construction undertaken for the state government.

Later discussion will also concern the reasons for considering household and local government final demand to be endogenous. A major point is that the level of these transactions in most cases can be considered as being a function of, or determined by the level of, local activity.

The transactions table itself tells a great deal about the economy. By studying Table VII it is possible to tell that, even though the value of minerals is greater, the economy is actually much more dependent upon agriculture. Only a small proportion of the mineral production income is spent locally. On the other hand, about two-thirds of the agricultural income is spent locally. The local household sector collects almost a third more from agriculture than from minerals.

In reviewing the nonlocal input section of the table, we note that factor earnings to nonresidents from the mineral industry are quite high. The implication to be drawn is that this is an area in which very little exploration work is being done although the mineral properties are producing. If exploration work were a large factor and mineral production not yet a large factor, this figure might well be negative.

Another fact the table reveals is that the manufacturing is largely the processing of agricultural products, since that industry makes a fairly large purchase from agriculture. However, there is also a fair amount of other manufacturing for which raw material must be imported, as shown by the size of import purchases.

Inspection of the transportation and utilities industry reveals that this area is not on a main transportation route, nor does it have major electrical or other utility plants. This is shown by the small amount appearing in the exogenous section of the table and the small amount of factor earnings leaving the economy.

A review of the trade industries indicates this activity to be locally oriented. A very small amount of wholesaling is done outside the area, but practically no retail or service sales are made to nonresidents, except to travelers. Wholesaling is not a big industry, and the retailers must import a large proportion of their supplies.

The direct sources of income payments to the household segments also give the analyst considerable information.

Thus, even aside from any further use, the input-output table is a useful tool of analysis. A careful study will reveal the essential characteristics of the Rawhide community system. Such examination is only cursory, however, and in order to make maximum use of the table, further manipulation is in order. As indicated in the non-numerical illustration (Table V), it is necessary to obtain the ratios $y_{ij}/Y_j = a_{ij}$ or input coefficients. In Table VIII each cell value is divided by the total input for the column in which it falls. For the first eleven rows and columns, the ratios are the same as they would be had they been calculated from total output, since, in this case, input equals output.

The decimal numbers in Table VIII indicate the amount of immediate purchases in cents made by the industry heading the column for each dollar of output produced by that industry. It is now possible to compare directly the purchasing patterns of various industries without taking into account their respective sizes. This table may also be viewed as reflecting the initial turnover of a new dollar in the system.

By studying the transaction and input coefficient tables, the analyst can learn much about the economic activity of a community. However, since a major concern is usually cause-and-effect relationships, attention must also be given to a third table—that representing $[I - A]^{-1}$.

In earlier discussion it was noted that the elements of this table (IX) show the amount of both direct and indirect activity produced for each industry (listed at the left) that results from one unit of basic income received by the industry listed at the top. Thus, one dollar received by agriculture for selling a farm product outside the community means a total of 1.00×1.1884 or $1.19 to the local agriculture industry. The one dollar is the original one received, while the 19 cents is produced from dollar turnover in the community. Similarly this original basic-income dollar produces indirectly $.27 for local retailers and one and a half cents in local government taxes.

TABLE VIII

INPUT COEFFICIENTS (BASED ON TABLE VII)

RAWHIDE AREA, U.S.A.

19 —

	Endogenous Transactions — Commercial and Producing Sector									Local Final Demand Sec.			Exogenous Transactions — Outside World Demand Sec.			
	1 Agr.	2 Min.	3 Const. Contr.	4 Manuf.	5 Trans. & Util.	6 Farm Product Handlers	7 Other Whls.	8 Retailers	9 All Serv.	10 Local Govt.	11 Local Hshld.	12 Sales to Local Invest.	13 Nonlocal Govt.	14 Travelers	15 Other	16 TOTAL SALES OR OUTPUT
1. Agriculture	.1130	-0-	-0-	.3980	-0-	.5528	.0018	.0019	-0-	-0-	-0-	-.0211	.1214	-0-	.2976	.1197
2. Minerals	-0-	.1056	-0-	-0-	.0588	-0-	-0-	-0-	-0-	-0-	-0-	-0-	-0-	-0-	.4466	.1215
3. Construction Contractors	.0017	.0811	.0620	.0014	.0017	.0003	.0007	.0013	.0049	.0025	.0026	.3431	.3784	-0-	-0-	.0306
4. Manufacturers	.0153	-0-	.0082	-0-	.0015	.0016	.0025	.0480	.0014	.0015	.0077	-0-	-0-	-0-	.1184	.0369
5. Transportation & Utilities	.0410	.0015	.0108	.0821	.0594	.0058	.0337	.0208	.0832	.0270	.0211	-0-	.0070	-0-	-0-	.0196
6. Farm Product Handlers	.0752	-0-	-0-	-0-	-0-	.0010	.0057	.1614	-0-	-0-	-0-	-0-	-0-	-0-	.0692	.0257
7. Other Wholesalers	.0377	.0145	.0123	.0015	.0160	.0219	.0192	.0084	.0738	.0392	.4804	.6780	.0029	.8038	.0055	.1099
8. Retailers	.0632	.0102	.0233	.0072	.0558	.0065	-0-	-0-	.0312	.0113	.1216	-0-	.0082	.1962	-0-	.0268
9. All Service	.0476	.0105	.0108	.0046	-0-	.0006	.0060	.0290	.0589	.0257	.0086	-0-	.0029	-0-	-0-	.0528
10. Local Government	.0225	.0259	.0033	-0-	-0-	.0045	.0044	.0085	.0142	-0-	-0-	-0-	.1743	-0-	-0-	.0198
11. Local Household	.2943	.2033	.2366	.0984	.2832	.0634	.0701	.1324	.3902	.6081	.0126	-0-	.3128	-0-	.0627	.1503
TOTAL ABOVE	.7115	.4026	.3673	.5952	.4994	.6584	.1441	.4117	.6761	.7153	.6546					.6876
12. Nonlocal Government	.0262	.0657	.0080	.0100	.0333	.0065	.0947	.0076	.0142	.0079	.1058					.0324
13. Nonlocal Factor Earnings	.0267	.3549	.0736	.0884	.1220	.2687	.0197	.0339	.1520	.0692	.0176					.0648
14. Capital Consumption	.1139	.1063	.0268	.0129	.1009	.0658	.0083	.0123	.0724	-0-	-0-					.0838
15. Imports	.1217	.0705	.5243	.3455	.2444	-0-	.7332	.5345	.0853	.0601	.1938					.1736
16. Other										.2075	.0201					.0083
TOTAL INPUT	1.0000	1.0000	1.0000	1.0000	1.0000	1.0000	1.0000	1.0000	1.0000	1.0000	1.0000	1.0000	1.0000	1.0000	1.0000	1.0000

TABLE IX

Direct and Indirect Activity Per Dollar of Export
Rawhide Area, U.S.A.
19 –

$$[I-A]^{-1}$$

	1 Agr.	2 Min.	3 Const. Contr.	4 Manuf.	5 Trans. & Utl.	6 Farm Product Handlers	7 Other Whls.	8 Retailers	9 All Serv.	10 Local Govt.	11 Local Hshld.
1. Agriculture	1.1884	.0012	.0053	.4676	.0019	.6498	.0039	.0247	.0040	.0040	.0139
2. Minerals	.0027	1.1171	.0009	.0067	.0703	.0019	.0025	.0023	.0066	.0028	.0026
3. Construction Contractors	.0044	.0386	1.0673	.0037	.0058	.0027	.0014	.0026	.0079	.0055	.0048
4. Manufacturers	.0320	.0078	.0177	1.0125	.0114	.0166	.0060	.0540	.0185	.0227	.0334
5. Transportation & Utilities	.0777	.0151	.0266	.1186	1.0823	.0468	.0414	.9433	.1164	.0593	.0448
6. Farm Product Handlers	.0883	-0-	.0002	.0333	-0-	1.0463	.0002	.0016	.0001	.0001	.0003
7. Other Wholesalers	.0848	.0370	.0378	.0338	.0447	.0888	1.0160	.1783	.0823	.0835	.0872
8. Retailers	.2745	.1412	.1589	.1510	.1825	.1638	.0645	1.1016	.3168	.3549	.5634
9. All Service	.1172	.0485	.0504	.0651	.0761	.0873	.0201	.0573	1.1036	.1024	.1593
10. Local Government	.0146	.0350	.0108	.0260	.0697	.0267	.0164	.0171	.0765	1.0162	.0255
11. Local Household	.4618	.2916	.3039	.3049	.4071	.3136	.1028	.2061	.5432	.7163	1.1722
TOTAL MULTIPLIER	2.3527	1.7331	1.6798	2.2232	1.9518	2.3943	1.2752	1.6889	2.2759	2.3677	2.1074

As another example, total exports by manufacturers produce indirectly \$7,651,000 × 0.1510 or \$1,155,000 in sales by retailers and \$7,651,000 × 0.3049 or \$2,333,000 in personal income to residents.

The Rawhide area will be used as an example throughout the remainder of this study to bring other intricacies of its economic structure to light.

Constant Input Coefficients

From a theoretical standpoint the input-output model requires each input for any one industry to be a linear homogeneous function of that industry's output. That is, for the jth industry, the ith input is $a_{ij}Y_j$ where a_{ij} is constant. This relationship can be plotted, as in Figure 1.

Often it is noted that a dollar increase in total output is not accompanied by a proportional increase in each input. The farmer's output depends on the weather; if the season is good his output may be high, but his costs would be similar to those for a poor season. Similarly, the retailer can increase his sales considerably without paying additional rent or consuming additional utility services. Likewise, the manufacturer can effect economies-of-scale in that he can often double his output yet incur only a small increase in overhead. Thus, at first glance the linear homogeneous function (or constant input) requirement appears extremely restricting.

In turning to economic systems in general, factors[1] working against the constant input coefficient requirement are: (1) economies-of-scale, (2) localization economies—external economies occurring to an industry as a result of like-producing units aggregating at one point, (3) urbanization economies—external economies resulting from unlike-producing units aggregating at one point, (4) relative price changes (it is considered here that inputs are measured in dollars), (5) substitution in inputs as prices and trading patterns change, and (6) technological change. Added to these are the inherent peculiarities of some industries in relating input to output. Of course, these same factors are of concern in constructing community multipliers.

FIGURE 1

A LINEAR HOMOGENEOUS FUNCTION

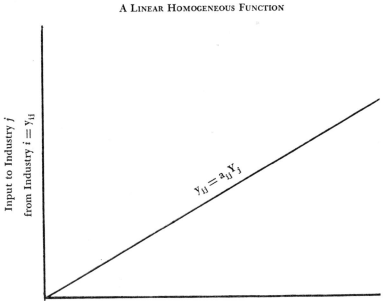

Input to Industry j from Industry $i = Y_{ij}$

$Y_{ij} = a_{ij} Y_j$

Total Output of Industry $j = Y_j$

At first glance, in view of the many factors working against constant input coefficients, there probably appears to be little merit in even considering an input-output model. At this point, however, only a small part of the picture is being examined.

It would be well to mention, first, that very few economic models exist that do not in some way rely on constant coefficients of some type. For example, the community multiplier, as a representation of the economic base concept, is merely a one-dimensional input-output model employing only one coefficient assumed to be constant—a much less realistic assumption than one in which individual industry coefficients are constant. Even if the researcher avoids the use of such models and attempts a less structured approach, he is still very possibly relying on constant coefficients in order to analyze his problem, but in an intuitive way. Thus, he loses the advantage of a carefully structured framework.

However, it must be recognized that many factors are also at work in an economic system (or, in some cases, society) that stabilize input coefficients. Of considerable importance are custom, habit, and inertia. If a manufacturer is satisfied with his supplier, why should he seek a new one just because business has increased? It takes time to introduce innovations; people prefer old familiar methods. New processes require considerable capital investment.

Another factor, which may appear at first glance to be working against stability of coefficients but which actually contributes to it, is the freedom of movement of people and businesses in response to new or better opportunities. The fact is that people take their habits and customary business practices with them. Another aspect is that this freedom of movement tends to lessen expansion by current local industries, thus limiting the effect of economies-of-scale. The relatively free movement of people means also that a doubling of community income may not mean any more money per capita than before, thus spending habits tend to remain stable. Implied in this discussion is the assumption that new people moving into the community will have essentially the same habits as those already in the community. The authors have noted that this is not always the case. Some new residents will be in a different social stratum, and their consumption patterns will be different. This change can be easily handled, however, as will be explained later.

In general, this in-movement of people and industries tends to bring the community to an equilibrium position rather quickly. A downward shift in basic income may require a longer adjustment period to reach equilibrium, but the mere existence of ghost towns attests to the final outcome of that adjustment.

Another important factor, as noted in Chapter II, is that there are also trading patterns centered around transportation costs for many products. Thus, the distance that coal, cement, building stone, and other such products can be profitably shipped is quite limited.

Also in Chapter II, considerable empirical evidence was given to support the contention that the constant input coefficient requirement is not unduly hard to live with. Some additional empirical evidence can be inserted at this point. In Table X is shown the relationship of the input characterized by payroll to output characterized by gross business of trade in the United States. In view of changes that have taken place in the nation, the stability of these ratios is quite remarkable.

TABLE X

RELATIONSHIP BETWEEN PAYROLLS AND GROSS BUSINESS
RETAIL AND WHOLESALE TRADE
— UNITED STATES —
1942 — 1961
(MILLIONS OF DOLLARS)

Year	Payroll	Gross	Payroll ÷ Gross Ratio
1942	10,971	91,516	.1199
1943	11,893	101,540	.1171
1944	12,971	111,712	.1161
1945	14,665	122,836	.1194
1946	19,560	162,392	.1204
1947	22,871	192,404	.1189
1948	25,298	211,819	.1194
1949	25,629	196,478	.1304
1950	27,322	214,272	.1275
1951	29,982	257,366	.1165
1952	31,773	268,422	.1183
1953	33,468	281,176	.1190
1954	34,447	278,243	.1238
1955	36,974	301,462	.1226
1956	40,001	316,690	.1263
1957	42,301	335,710	.1260
1958	43,060	333,553	.1291
1959	46,255	350,016	.1322
1960	49,073	367,627	.1335
1961	49,997	369,528	.1352

Source: Various issues, *Survey of Current Business*, U. S. Department of Commerce.

The arguments given here do not mean that the authors do not recognize that coefficients do change over time. Where forecasts are made, it is quite often necessary to take into account possible changes. These are then inserted into the model before multiplying by the expected new export vector. Actually, the problem in that case is not in trying to overcome the constant input coefficient requirement; it is in trying to determine how coefficients will vary or what their values will be at certain points in time. Many economists criticize the assumption of constancy in input coefficients without adding much information about how they change. This is an area that admittedly needs more work.

In some cases in which the project objective requires a manipulative model rather than one in which coefficients are simply changed for particular predictive periods, the basic input-output model can be changed, as:

$$Y_i = \sum_j y_{ij} + z_i$$

but where now

$$y_{ij} = a_{ji}Y_j + c_{ij}$$

instead of simply

$$y_{ij} = a_{ij}Y_j.$$

Here c_{ij} is a constant, denoting input to the jth industry from the ith industry regardless of the jth industry's output. Such a function is plotted in Figure 2.

FIGURE 2

A SIMPLE LINEAR FUNCTION

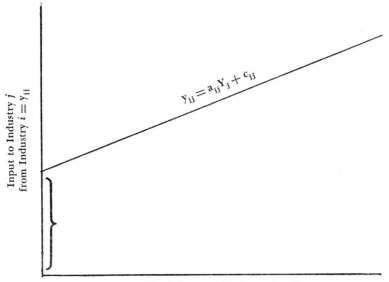

Input to Industry j from Industry $i = y_{ij}$

$y_{ij} = a_{ij}Y_j + c_{ij}$

Total Output of Industry $j = Y_j$

To start with, we may say that

$$Y_i \geqq \sum_j^n c_{ij}$$

or that output of the jth industry can never be lower than its constant input (or, in essence, nothing can be produced from something).

In writing the model in matrix form and in letting B represent an $n \times 1$ vector in which each element equals $\sum_j c_{ij}$, we have

$$Y = AY + B + Z$$

and $\quad Y = [I - A]^{-1} Z + [I - A]^{-1} B$

In writing $[I - A]^{-1} B$ as K, an n dimensional column vector, we have

$$Y = [I - A]^{-1} Z + K$$

Now it can be seen that the lower limit of each Y_i is the corresponding element k_i rather than $\sum_j^n c_{ij}$. Actually, these lower limits would be of no significance if the researchers picked realistic values of c_{ij} for the values of Y_i expected to be confronted. Many different combinations of a_{ij} and c_{ij} could be used in order to, in essence, obtain any input function desired. In practice, it is expected that the c_{ij} would often be taken as zero, so that the more conventional input-output model is used for all but a few highly critical interrelationships.

CHAPTER IV

Local Industry Delineation
and Measurement Units

THE INPUT-OUTPUT MODEL defined in Chapter III makes two specific demands concerning local industry delineation: (1) input coefficients must remain constant and (2) sales by any particular industry to all other industries must be handled in identically defined units. As already discussed, the first requirement indicates that input of all raw materials, supplies, power, and workforce must vary in direct proportion to output for any particular industry. The second requirement says that barrels of oil cannot be added to gallons when talking about the output of the oil industry.

In addition to the theoretical requirements of the model, another major criterion pertaining to industry delineation and measurement units is *understandability*. People use the results of economic analyses; if the results cannot be communicated and put to use, the analyses are of no value. Thus, an axiom is submitted: To the extent permitted by theoretical requirements and the objectives of the study, delineate industries and define measurement units in terms most commonly understood and used.

Of course, many other considerations are involved in local industry delineation and selection of measurement units. Of considerable concern is the availability of secondary data. Simplification of field work should also be taken into account.

For an input-output model, the authors strongly prefer current value dollar data of a gross receipts nature as the major measurement unit. This does not preclude the use of other units in special circumstances.

Emphasis in this chapter will now be turned to the many considerations involved in setting up industry classes for an input-output model. An actual classification found to be of general value is submitted and particular measurement units are defined.

Consideration is also given to the problem of separating endogenous and exogenous transactions.

Constant Input Coefficients and the Aggregation Problem

While the theoretical input-output model requires constant input coefficients, it must be recognized that such a requirement is never completely fulfilled in practice. Most community analyses are undertaken because change is occurring, has occurred, or is anticipated. Consequently, the economy most in need of analysis may also be the one least likely to fill completely this requirement of the input-output model.

The particular aggregation of community economic activity into industries for use in the analysis has considerable bearing on the extent to which the constant input coefficient requirement is met. As an example, let us consider a situation in a mining community where there are both open-pit and underground mines. Owing to technological change a vast conversion to more economical open-pit methods is made possible in the current underground mining industry. The researcher analyzing this situation would naturally consider the pending change in his aggregating procedures. He would probably want to have separate groupings of open-pit and underground mines in order to rely on constancy of input for each process rather than on constancy for all mining.

However, if the researcher has reason to believe that underground production would expand at a comparable rate to open-pit production, he may not need to handle the two industries separately in order to maintain constancy. The point is that components of the economy which might change in relative output quite drastically in the future and whose input factors are quite different should not be aggregated into one industry.

Some researchers feel that only businesses producing the same product or service should be placed together. The authors agree, but with certain qualifications. The goal should be to aggregate into one industry only those activities whose changes in output rate are apt to be highly correlated. An example would be the aggregation of local wholesaling and retailing, since they tend to be highly correlated.

The objectives of the study and the funds available also often control the grouping. For example, it might be deemed advisable to make separate aggregations of various facets of retailing—eating and drinking places, auto supply firms, and agricultural supply houses—if the objectives of the survey include a minute analysis of the travel industry. On the other hand, such aggregation might not contribute significantly to the analysis if travel were not a consideration. In that case, budgetary considerations might dictate aggregation of all retailing into one industry.

Even though all activities are stratified into the most practical industry categories from the standpoint of likely future changes, some instability of coefficients will often remain. If the model is to be used in measuring the future effect of change, aggregate into an industry those groups for which adjustments are most simple.

In summary, it should be said that good analytical results depend quite heavily upon the particular aggregations used. The classification system should be designed with possible future changes, project objectives, idiosyncrasies of certain industries, and project funds in mind.

LOCAL INDUSTRY DELINEATION

The following classification represents about minimal breakdown for most community economic systems. Since each such economy has its own peculiarities and since there are differences in study objectives, deviations from these particular listings can be expected. If, for example, one of these industries constitutes a very minor part of the over-all economic activity, it might well be combined with another segment. On the other hand, it may be desirable to make further breakdowns of some of the industry classes.

The authors have given consideration to three factors in setting up the classification: (1) requirements of the economic model for validity, (2) needs of the typical user of community economic analyses, and (3) available sources of data.

The definitions for each industry agree with those published in the Standard Industrial Classification Manual.[1] For some businesses, classification may be difficult, for example, a manufacturer who is also a retailer. The most commonly used method is the assignment of the business to the grouping that is most consistent with its major activity. If the retail end of a bakery constitutes about one-third of its business, it is still a manufacturing concern. A doughnut shop selling largely at retail would be a retailer. In short, a firm's functions cannot be split between two categories. Using this approach to classification will greatly reduce data handling and make the results more useful. Its effect on stability of the model will not be serious.

Agricultural (S.I.C. Division A), excluding services. In most areas agriculture will have a sufficient volume of activity to be considered as a separate industry. Most agricultural enterprises are fairly small, although they are becoming larger each year. Their purchasing pattern is quite distinct, and their orientation toward the local economy is usually quite strong.

There is usually no problem in determining distinctness, although florists and greenhouses sometimes pose problems. Inclusion of the latter would depend upon whether production, wholesaling, or retailing dominates in the particular firm. Production would be considered an agricultural enterprise.

Output, or sales, entries in the table can usually be quite easily defined by taking gross receipts at the point of sale plus changes in inventory. The latter can be considered an exogenous transaction, since only current activity is termed endogenous. Transportation charges paid by the farmer would be included in the sales figure and considered later in payments to the transportation sector by agriculture. Incentive payments received from the federal government can be included as a sale to government, even though no actual sale is made. Such a sales definition is compatible with that used by the Bureau of the Census in the Census of Agriculture and similarly agrees with U.S. Department of Agriculture data.

One difficulty arises in the use of U.S. Department of Agriculture market receipts data—farm-to-farm sales are not reported unless there is a movement across a state line. An integral part of the workings of a community economic system is "within" industry sales. Inclusion of such sales is also often more clear to users of the results. Thus, even where good secondary data are available, the researcher must often add to those data to show the complete picture.

At times it is useful to break agriculture into types. This will usually depend upon the general objectives of the survey. For example, a study made of an area dominated by agricultural activity may involve analysis of changes in intensive irrigation, dry land crop production, and cattle ranching. Since input patterns of each of these are usually quite different, there would be strong justification for three separate classifications. This is especially true if fairly drastic changes are occuring or are expected in volume of output in one of these types of agriculture. Such changes would upset constancy of input in the total agricultural picture. Usually, however, changes in agriculture are quite slow and no particular problem develops from viewing it as a whole.

Minerals (S.I.C. Division B). In those economies where mineral production is of significance it should be given a separate row and column in the transactions table.

The purchasing patterns of minerals industries are usually quite different from those of other industries. Large outlays are usually made initially in exploration, purchasing of rights, and developing the mine or drilling the well. A large proportion of subsequent income from production then goes to amortize the initial investment. Equipment and supply needs are often obtained outside the community in which they operate, but usually considerable amounts are spent locally for labor and utilities.

A satisfactory measure of sales for most studies is to be found in U.S. Bureau of Mines reports on value of minerals produced. Value of product is determined at the mine or wellhead so that no transportation costs are involved. In cases where a processing mill is directly associated with the mine, value is usually taken on the processed product. In this case some transportation costs may be involved. These data are compiled for states and, in some instances, for counties. In addition to product value, mining companies often perform services or contract work for other companies. Since this is a part of the economic activity of the area, it should be treated as income and expenditure in the table.

In some studies it may be desirable to divide mineral production into groups, such as open-pit mining, underground mining, oil and gas production, and mineral services. The expenditure pattern of each of these is quite different, hence a change in output rate of one of them not accompanied by a near-equal change in the others could destroy the constant input situation for the over-all industry. If any or all of these categories are very important to the community being studied, some sort of breakdown should be attempted.

Exploration and mineral service activities are very often made a separate category if they are of significance to the over-all analysis. Their economic activity has to be measured in something besides value of minerals produced, since they ordinarily produce none. A simple gross receipts measure is usually quite satisfactory. An especially important consideration in determining whether this group should or should not be separated from the actual producers hinges on the source of receipts. If they represent investment from outside the area for exploration purposes and have little relation to current production activities, then the mineral service industry should certainly be treated separately from production. However, at other times mineral service firm activities may be directly related to current production and can then be easily combined with the producing industry. Of course, no separation is needed if exploration activities are too minor to warrant consideration.

Construction Contractors (S.I.C. Division C). Included in this category are firms engaged in new construction, additions, alterations, and repairs. It covers three broad types of activity: (1) building construction by general contractors; (2) other (usually heavy) construction by general contractors; and (3) construction by special trade contractors; that is, carpenters, plumbers, electricians, and painters. Generally speaking, firms operating within the local economy, regardless of headquarters, should be included.

Sales include receipts from all construction jobs in the local area being studied. Such a measure should compare closely to "value of construction completed" during the period, plus repair and service sales, and subcontracting. Receipts by local firms for work done in other areas are specifically excluded. This is a somewhat arbitrary ruling, but it does overcome definitional problems regarding which operations are "local" in character and the consequential problem of associating local purchases with local sales.

Capital expenditures in most communities are only indirectly linked to the level of current operations. Instead, such investment is the product of long-range plans and expected future growth. Since most construction-contractor activity falls into the class of capital investment, a large amount of the receipts by contractors would be expected to fall into the exogenous segment of the table. Only sales associated with repairs would generally be classed as endogenous. These points will be pursued in greater detail later.

Considerations of constancy in coefficients often make it advisable to establish two or more groups of contractors. Heavy construction contractors often have very different purchase and sales habits from general building contractors. Special trade contractors, consisting largely of individuals and small firms, also have their peculiarities. If any one or all of these types are of considerable importance in a community, and especially if there is likelihood of either major growth or decline in some of them, they probably should be treated as separate industries.

Manufacturing (S.I.C. Division D). Every community economic system has a certain number of bakeries, dairies, print shops, and slaughterhouses that produce for the local market. Some of these may make extensive sales to export also. In addition, there are plants whose market orientation is almost wholly to the outside. The researcher will necessarily consider this situation in determining the wisdom of setting up two or even more manufacturing categories.

Gross receipts appears to be the most appropriate measure for manufacturing, even though it is customary to consider "value added" when speaking of this industry. It is important that information in all cells of the model be comparable. In the relationship of other industries to this one, value added concepts would not be comparable, and it is doubtful that information could easily be gathered on that basis. Questions about purchases from manufacturing would almost always be answered on a gross value basis.

Gross sales figures should exclude transportation charges for products leaving the plant and should be net after deductions or discounts. If the firm does some retailing and wholesaling of its products, those margins will be included in gross sales. Any service sales would necessarily be included also. Such an output measure is closely comparable to "value of shipments" used in the U.S. Census of Manufacturers.

Transportation and Utilities (S.I.C. Division E). The types of firms included in this group are almost always of importance in the community. They also have input coefficients distinctly different from other business categories. This industry is closely tied to most other industries in the community system.

The recommended measure of sales (output) by the transportation and utilities industry consists of local area receipts from sales of any services or commodities, less returns and allowances. For the other industries discussed so far, total output has included the value of any exports. This industry, however, has certain peculiarities that make it advisable to *exclude exports.*

The peculiarities stem from the fact that the industry is dominated by firms having geographically widespread operations. When the community in question lies on a transcontinental or other long route, local expenditures directly associated with local operations of the company may be minor compared to local expenditures for servicing the larger operation. For example, it is possible for a transportation or utility company to pay out more for payrolls in a particular community than it receives in revenue.

In order to handle this problem, it is suggested that all local purchases for this industry be divided into two columns, one reflecting those directly associated with local receipts and the other showing expenditures connected with maintaining the "through" service. The purchases associated with local receipts would then be classed as endogenous transactions; all other purchases would make up an exogenous transactions column representing export sales by other local industries. Some difficulty may be experienced in making such a separation; a method sometimes used is the allocation, based upon the ratio of total receipts to local area receipts, of the expenditures provided in national or regional reports of the company. For example, a local wood processor who sells telephone poles to a company that maintains long-distance lines would be selling some of them to the local utilities industry and exporting the rest. The telephone company payroll would appear partially as local purchases from households and partially as exports of services by the household sector. The same approach would apply for every local purchase.

In the collection of data, it is quite often necessary to separate utilities from transportation. Receipts by utility companies are fairly easy to determine. Transportation is a much more heterogeneous group, and problems of definition arise. As an example, it is sometimes difficult to determine just who is paying transportation costs on a product that is shipped out of the community. We have found that there are some advantages in regarding value of sales by mining and manufacturing concerns as "at the plant." Thus, these sales would not include shipping costs. Reasons for this decision were discussed previously and are directly connected with availability of secondary information.

In general, it seems safe to assume that all transportation costs are paid by the receiver of the goods. This assumption would enforce the constraint that in order for a transportation payment to be a local sale, the receiver would have to be a resident of the community. Such a constraint works out for most businesses. Agriculture is an exception, however, since available data on sales assume that the farmer or rancher pays transportation to the point of sale. Whether or not this is actually an exception depends upon the consideration of the "point of sale" concept. If the plant is considered the point of sale for other products, this figuring of farm costs could be considered to fit into the pattern somewhat.

Wholesaling (S.I.C. Division F, Major Group 50). Wholesaling should be handled as a separate industry in most community economic analyses, especially where they do considerable export selling. Wholesalers usually perform much less service per dollar of sales than do retailers. Where they are of particular importance and especially where they may be serving a fairly large area outside of the one being analyzed, combining them with retailers could bias the analysis considerably. Even where they serve only local retailers, a separation of wholesaling can add to clarity.

For most community economic analyses, the most convenient sales figure to obtain is the gross sales figure for wholesale trade as reported by the U.S. Census of Business. This figure includes all receipts from sale of commodities and services less deductions for return of merchandise and discounts. All taxes collected by the wholesaler are included.

In agriculturally oriented economies, the farm product class of wholesalers should be separated from others. One of the strongest reasons for this is the fact that, so far as the local economy is concerned, these firms do not qualify as wholesalers because they deal with agriculture from both the buying and selling standpoint instead of with local retailers. There is often strong argument for including them in the agricultural sector as part of the marketing setup. For most purposes, they should probably be treated as a separate segment.

Another problem arises in minerals-oriented communities. Industrial supply houses, including oil field and mining supply, are treated as wholesalers by the census. Since their function is quite distinct from that usually considered to be wholesaling, they must be treated separately.

(*The Use of Trade Margins.*) The need for separating the two groups mentioned above from the regular wholesale category brings up a point for discussion here.

In some input-output analyses, particularly those involving the nation or large regions, only the trade margins are considered in the sales of wholesalers and retailers. The transactions table shows the user of the product purchasing directly from the manufacturer but supplying each trade sector with its necessary trade margin. The reason for this can probably be explained through an example. Most national models emphasize household consumption. The household sector is usually placed "outside the model," that is, it is treated as an autonomous sector in an open model. This treatment bypasses the constant input coefficient requirement of the model for the household sector.

Using such a model, suppose that at a certain time in the future it is expected that gasoline consumption by consumers will double and the purchase of apparel will be cut in half. Further suppose that the shifts are of equal magnitude so that total consumption remains identical. The actual result would be an approximate doubling of gasoline sales by refineries and a substantial reduction in sales by apparel manufacturers.

If only one trading sector were being used in the model to describe the economy and if all consumption dollars were routed first to the trading sector and then to the producing sectors, that input-output model would fail to describe the results of the change in consumption. That is, since the total consumption remained constant, the model would indicate no change. This sort of situation can be overcome by using only the trading margin as sales by the trading sector and by having the reflection of changes in consumer purchases come directly from the producer to the consumer.

This sort of problem is very seldom of much concern in the analysis of a community economic system. Small communities import a large proportion of consumer goods and export most of their production. Thus, the long series of vertical relationships from producer to consumer are seldom found. However, in larger communities and even occasionally in smaller ones some aspects of this type of problem are confronted. The simplest way to deal with it is to set up such separate grouping within the trade sector as is necessary to explain significant changes in any one sector.

Retailing (S.I.C. Division F, except Group 50). Except for the rare occasion when wholesaling is so insignificant that it can be combined with this sector, retailing should be treated as a separate industry. Sales as defined in the U.S. Census of Business—Retail Trade, appears to be the best output measure to use. This definition includes all money received from sale of commodities and service net after discounts and deductions for return of merchandise. All local and state sales taxes and federal excise taxes collected by the retailer for later disposition to the government or to be passed on to the wholesaler are included.

In some local economies where retailers do considerable export selling, such as sales to travelers and tourists, it is often well to set up several retail industries such as eating and drinking places, gasoline retailers, souvenir shops, and "all other." In a heavily agricultural area the analyst may want to consider farm supply stores separately.

Services (S.I.C. Division G and H plus agricultural services from Division A). This industry grouping includes such types of business as lodging, personal services, repairs, medical and health, business, professional, and finance plus nonprofit institutions and such government commercial operations as post offices. Government hospitals are in the medical group. The finance group, including banks, finance companies, and real estate and insurance companies, is often treated as a separate industry, since it is more strongly oriented toward serving the business sector than are other service industries which serve the consumer quite largely. In those areas where vacationers are heavy contributors to the basic income, lodging and vacation service industries such as dude ranches may be considered separately.

We have had some difficulty deciding upon the exact nonprofit institutions to include with this group. Those who conduct commercial ventures such as bars, restaurants, dancing, etc., are definitely included. Churches and some strictly service-type clubs may fit better into the household category. This decision produces no great effect on the model and can be related to the local condition by the researcher.

Sales data for the service industry include all receipts from sales of services and goods (including contributions to nonprofit organizations by members) less discounts and allowances for returned items. Sales by financial institutions include income from fees, interest, commissions, service charges, and any other payment for service.

The U.S. Census of Business—Selected Services data cover only a segment of the service industry. Medical and health, professional, and financial services are not covered, for example. This makes it necessary to survey these groups rather carefully, since no aggregate sales data can be obtained from secondary sources.

Local Government (S.I.C. Division I, Major Group 93). All local government units, such as counties, cities, school districts, and special districts, are included in this group. This should be a separate industry in just about every analysis, owing to its peculiar purchasing pattern, which emphasizes money movement to the "household sector," that is, payrolls and welfare type payments. In an analysis at less than the state level, state government would be excluded here.

In order to stay with concepts used in constructing the national income accounts, it is recommended that government "enterprises" be included with business segments rather than with government. Such enterprises are those government agencies whose operating costs are, at least to a substantial extent, covered through the sale of goods and services. Thus, post offices and most hospitals should be classed as service industries, and public power, water, and sanitary systems as utilities.

"Sales" by local government consist of all revenue, regardless of source, that is, taxes, fees, licenses, fines, interest, and transfer payments from nonlocal governments. Receipts from issuance of debt, recoupment of loans, and sale of investments are not counted as "sales." Later discussion on the handling of investment will clarify this point.

For this category we have somewhat arbitrarily decided to deviate from a prior general recommendation of including all interindustry transactions as sales. The closeness with which local government units work together is considered reason enough to exclude from the transactions table transfers of funds among such units, as taxes and fees collected by one governmental unit for others. For example, in some states, counties collect all property taxes and apportion them among the other units. Sometimes justice-of-the-peace fines go to the school districts. Often, counties collect property taxes on behalf of the state and the state collects excise taxes, such as that on tobacco, that it remits directly to local governments.

We suggest that these taxes be regarded as revenue only to the unit to which they are sent. The criterion used is that receipts constitute revenue only if they are "controllable" or "spendable" by the unit receiving them. Thus, cigarette taxes collected by the State of Wyoming on behalf of the cities and counties in which sales took place are actually the property of the cities and counties. The state is allowed to deduct collection expenses only. On the other hand, taxes collected by the state for use in the school foundation program are state money, even though the school districts eventually get most of it, because the state determines how it will be distributed to them.

In case the community economic system is considered to cover an entire state, state government can be treated as another unit of local government. In that case all fund transfers between state and local governments can be considered internal transactions.

Household. For the analysis of community economic systems a "household" industry is required to handle all receipts by residents of the community. These people may be thought of as selling their labor skills and managerial talents for salaries, wages, profits, royalties, etc.

In most instances "sales" by the household industry is most easily defined as realized personal income received by residents of the community. The "realized" qualification is made to avoid using imputed items included by the U.S. Department of Commerce in their series. They specify that personal income is all current income received by residents from all sources, inclusive of transfers from government and business but exclusive of transfers among persons.[2]

The word "residents," as defined here, means individuals, plus some nonprofit institutions (not included in the service industry), private trust funds, and other private health or welfare funds. Nonprofit institutions included would be churches, social clubs, labor organizations, nonprofit and nongovernment schools, and charitable organizations. Any nonprofit institution carrying on commercial operations would be classified in the service group.

Current income to these residents includes that received from both inside and outside the local economy. Personal income created within the local economy but paid to other than local residents is excluded.

SPECIAL HANDLING OF DOMINANT LOCAL INDUSTRIES

In many areas where community economic analysis may be considered to be of value, there will be a few individual businesses that dominate the economic activity. Manufacturing plants and mines are most often in this category. Where such situations exist, it is well, for the sake of stability of input co-efficients, to treat each of these as a separate industry in the analysis.

This often brings up the problem of disclosure. In assuming that written consent to disclose operations could not be obtained from these industries or that other reasons exist for their not disclosing operations, the analysis can be completed on a separate basis; but, when it comes time to publish results, these dominant industries should be collapsed with other industries throughout the report. Thus, the requirements of input-output analysis can be met, but the operations of these firms need not be disclosed.

As an example, suppose an analysis were being made of an area dominated by the operations of a copper mine. In making a superficial check of the area, it is found that there are other smaller mining operations on gold and silver ores in the area plus a considerable activity in oil and gas production. By combining operations of all minerals, it is possible to cover up operations of the copper mine sufficiently.

ENDOGENOUS-EXOGENOUS SALES

So far, in this chapter, emphasis has been given to the problems of selecting a measure of sales to be used in each industry and proper classification of local firms into industries. Attention will now be turned to the model itself and the designation of those transactions to be considered local current activity (endogenous to the model) and those that provide basic income or denote trading activity with the outside world (exogenous to the model). Our emphasis now swings away from industries, as such, to sales transactions.

In earlier discussion it was indicated that only current operational transactions among local industries are to be considered endogenous to the model. Identity of the seller has no bearing on that classification, but the requirement that it be "among local industries" definitely eliminates purchases by industries operating outside of the model.

One of the first requirements, therefore, is to define the term "local industries." To a large degree this has been done in the discussion of classification. The endogenous section of the model is the only one that requires industry classification. Sometimes it is convenient to make some classification of exogenous activity, but this is a matter of preference on the part of the particular analyst. All industries operating in the community plus local government and the household sector are to be regarded as local industries.

Listing the trading, producing, and service businesses operating in the community as local industries is self-explanatory. The reasons for including local government and household may not be so clear. Local governments have been observed by the authors to have expenditure patterns closely associated with revenue. Since a major part of revenue comes from local sources, the expenditure patterns are quite sensitive to economic changes in the community. This places local governments on a comparable basis with many types of local business.

In contrast, the local purchasing patterns of nonlocal government units have very little correlation with local revenue. Decisions by one of these units to spend money in a community are based upon considerations that have little to do with the amount of tax revenue received from that community. For that reason, all transactions related to nonlocal government units are considered to be exogenous even though a local office may be maintained. Their local expenditures constitute basic income to the industry selling the supplies or services.

Arguments for considering household-related transactions as exogenous in input-output models on the national scale are based on the observations that actual consumer purchases often vary significantly from disposable income and that this is an important cause of fluctuations in economic activity levels. Observations on the local level indicate that consumer purchasing generally follows disposable income reasonably closely in comparison with other changes usually affecting the local economy. One important factor causing the difference between national and local patterns is the constant migration of people according to economic opportunity. It is also important to note that usually the community economy for which an analysis is needed is already involved in economic changes that are far more significant than can be attributed to casual changes in consumer purchasing patterns. In consequence, for a short time period there is little to be lost by including households in the model. The advantages of treating household interaction by means of the model far outweigh any possible disadvantages.

Once the local industries are defined, attention can be paid to particular transactions by these local industries. Generally speaking, endogenous transactions by a particular firm will be those chargeable as expenses of operation during the current period for income tax purposes. These would include local purchases of raw materials, supplies, commodities for resale, and other expense items. Any of these purchased from nonlocal firms would, of course, constitute an import.

There is some argument about short-term capital expenditures. The point involved here is whether such purchases are made from current local revenue or from savings or borrowed funds. In some special cases the analyst may wish to define some capital expenditures as endogenous.

In the determination of national income accounts, only purchases of houses by householders are considered capital investment; all other durable goods purchases are treated as current consumption. We subscribe to this same distinction for most community studies. However, it has been noted that housing construction is often somewhat related to the level of current local activity or, in essence, to the level of household income.

As indicated previously, clarity may be added to the exogenous sector by classifying these transactions. One such division that has proven useful is: (1) sales to local investment, (2) sales to nonlocal government agencies, (3) sales to visitors or tourists, (4) other outside world sales, and (5) income to residents from the outside world. These divisions are dictated by analysis only, and not by any requirement of the model.

The sales-to-local-investment class would include a net change in agriculture inventories, sales of capital equipment to local industries, housing construction, and all other construction not regarded as repairs or part of current operation. It would not include sales of household appliances to individual households. In most cases, inventory change by sectors other than agriculture can be ignored. The column would include cost of mine development, exploration work, and oil well drilling. Thus, this group would encompass all local investment, excepting that involving a move of actual capital goods into the community from outside it.

Sales to visitors or tourists include purchases of auto supplies, food, lodging, souvenirs, services, and anything else purchased by travelers.

Income to local residents from the "outside world" should be treated as an "export" by the household sector. This grouping includes dividends, rents, interest, pensions, and all transfer payments, where these are received from sources outside of the community.

NONLOCAL INPUT (IMPORTS)

As noted in Chapter III, in developing the input-output model, nonlocal inputs (or, in essence, imports) are not a functional part of the model. These transactions need not be estimated. Yet, from an analysis standpoint, there is much to be gained by a breakdown and analysis of this group. In the example model (Tables VII and VIII), four nonlocal input classes are listed:

1. Nonlocal government
2. Nonlocal factor earnings
3. Capital consumption
4. Imports

This particular breakdown enables a community income-product account to be constructed. The analyst may desire other classes, however.

Nonlocal Government. These inputs denote payments by local industries in the form of taxes. All noncorporate income taxes are assumed to be paid by the household sector. Any taxes paid by the business itself, such as occupation taxes, property taxes, sales taxes, gasoline taxes, and employment taxes, would appear in the respective business columns. Local governments also pay employment tax. Corporate income tax is not included here, so that this row is defined similarly to "indirect business and non-tax liability" as treated in national income accounting, plus employment taxes.

Nonlocal Factor Earnings. This row includes current operational profit—before taxes—going to corporations (except strictly local corporations), interest paid by residents on financial paper held by nonresidents of the community, rent paid to outside interests, and any proprietorship profit not going to local persons. In some small communities all corporation profit and all mortgage interests can be included for the sake of simplicity.

These definitions will conform with "national income accounts" methods and will assist in the construction of an "area income and product measure."

Capital Consumption. This row is set up to handle items that, on an income statement, would be classified as depreciation. Accidental damage to fixed property not covered by insurance may also be included. Depletion allowances on natural resources are not included since the value of corresponding discoveries cannot be considered as income. Instead, the amount usually deducted for depletion should be added to factor income. This is also in accordance with methods used in the "national income accounts."

Other Imports. This is a catch-all row, but would consist primarily of payments made for inputs coming from the "outside world."

DETERMINING COMMUNITY INCOME-PRODUCT

Many researchers consider a measure of community income and product, similar in concept to the income-product account for the nation, to be of considerable value in studying a community economy. Such measures are especially of value in comparing the progress of a community from year to year, since the many duplications in the usually available transactions series are eliminated. Only by use of such a measure can "real" production in one community be compared to that of another community or the nation.

The input-output framework as developed in this book is in agreement with the usually accepted concepts of income and product measures. Consequently, such measures can easily be developed from the data included in input-output tables constructed along the lines suggested. This is not to imply that income-product accounts can only be constructed for a community by first developing an input-output table. Nevertheless, it must be recognized that much of the data required for an income-product account are identical to that required by an input-output table. Since stratified survey procedures are often desirable, the input-output table, by imposing a rigid discipline on the various strata, can be of considerable value in any income-product endeavor.

Before proceeding into actual construction of an income-product account, we shall review briefly the concepts behind such measures. First, a community may be considered as a producing entity or device. In turning out a product, it consumes raw materials, human services, and capital. The value of the product produced is reckoned to be of identical value to the raw materials, human services, and capital consumed. That is, something can never be produced from nothing.

Now, since the community economy is regarded as the producing entity, only sales made outside that entity would be accounted for. Likewise, only input from outside would be measured. For this concept both capital and human services are assumed to come from without the producing entity. The value of raw materials being consumed is identical to the value of imports, since internal transactions are not recognized.

Gross community product is defined as the value of output by this producing entity less the value of imports or raw materials coming from outside the entity. That is, gross community product is the "value added" by the producing entity. If capital consumption is also subtracted from the value of product produced, *net community product* is determined.

On the expenditure side of the producing entity's ledger, the receipts from sales are paid out as expenses for use of human services and capital consumption. The amount paid for human services constitutes net community income; upon including the capital consumption cost, charges against gross community product are obtained.

Table XI illustrates production activity within a community in the form of such an account.

TABLE XI

A SAMPLE PRODUCT-INCOME ACCOUNT

Human Service Expense	$30,000	Total Sales by Entity	$70,000
Capital Consumption	10,000	Less: Imports	30,000
Charges Against Gross Entity Product	$40,000	Gross Entity Product	$40,000

Considerable simplification must certainly be admitted in Table XI. From a somewhat more realistic viewpoint, "human services" would perhaps be better defined as "factors of production." Land owners receive rent; laborers are paid salaries and wages; and capital owners receive interest, dividends, and profit. The existence of governments must be recognized; these are paid in the form of taxes for their services.

Now, in turning to an input-output table quantification of a community economy, for example, that of the Rawhide area, it can be seen that most data are available. Sales by the producing sector of the economy would consist of the column totals for outside world demand. To this must be added total purchases of goods and services from the producing sector by households and by local government. These latter two can be obtained by taking the column total showing total outlay and subtracting such nonconsumption items as savings, investments, and tax payments. Imports by local government and household may be subtracted immediately from these total outlays, or these imports may be included within the total import figure to be subtracted from all the above community sales figures.

The alternative was used in the income-product account included as Table XII. As may be seen here, transfer payments by nonlocal government to local government are subtracted from the nonlocal government column total; earnings received by local residents from production activity outside the community are removed. However, payments received by residents from nonlocal government are not removed. At this point the reader would

TABLE XII

REALIZED INCOME-PRODUCT ACCOUNT

RAWHIDE AREA, U.S.A.

(IN THOUSANDS OF DOLLARS)

Compensation to Household:
Household Total Income $40,335
Less: Nonlocal Earnings By Residents (−) 4,053
Total Local Compensation $36,282
Factor Earnings to Nonresidents: $17,243
REALIZED NET INCOME $53,525

Business Taxes:
Paid to Local Government $2,749
Paid to Nonlocal Government 4,387
Total Business Taxes $ 7,136

Capital Consumption $ 9,080
CHARGES AGAINST GROSS COMMUNITY PRODUCT $69,741

Personal Consumption Expenditures:
Household Total Outlay $40,335
Less: Local Government Tax (−) 348
Nonlocal Government Tax (−) 4,266
Savings (−) 328
Housing Investment (−) 810
Total Personal Consumption $34,583

Local Government Purchase of Goods and Services:
Local Government Total Outlay $ 5,300
Less: Nonlocal Government Tax (−) 42
Savings & Investment (−) 1,100
Total Purchases of Goods & Services $ 4,158

Net Exogenous Demand on Community Economy:
Sales to Local Investment $ 4,742
Local Outlay by Nonlocal Government $12,640
Less: Transfer to Local Government (−) 2,203
$10,437
Nonlocal Traveler's Purchases 1,820
Other Transactions $64,621
Less: Nonlocal Earnings by Residents (−) 4,053
$60,568
Net Exogenous Demand $77,567
Less: Imports (−) 46,567
REALIZED GROSS COMMUNITY PRODUCT $69,741

probably find it helpful to trace each credit entry in Table XII to its source, Table VII, Rawhide Area Monetary Transactions. The debit side of Table XII is obtained by moving horizontally in the transactions table. The first entry is total realized personal income by the household sector less earnings received from nonlocal production activity. When factor earnings to nonresidents are added, realized net community income is obtained. All business taxes are obtained from the appropriate rows and entered (endogenous row 10 and exogenous nonlocal government). As explained earlier, all taxes on profits, whether corporate or personal, are assumed to be paid by stockholders and owners of factors of production not by the industry. Add to net community income total business taxes and the total of the capital consumption to obtain total charges against realized gross community product.

The qualification "realized" is added in describing this income-product account since imputed items commonly included in national accounts are omitted. If the researcher wishes to include such items, they can be added into the total household income on the debit side and the total household consumption on the credit side.

To a considerable extent the concepts involved in constructing the U.S. product-income accounts have been followed here. One exception is the exclusion of imputed items. Output here is defined in terms of the factors of production physically located within the community economy, while in the national accounts output is defined to be that accruing to factors of production supplied by U.S. residents despite their physical location. In line with this distinction, outside world earnings by residents were removed, but local earnings going to nonresidents were included in net community income.

Of course, many other less significant differences in concept exist between the U.S. product-income accounts and the suggested community account. These can be determined most easily by referring to the discussion concerning the definition of various industries or transactions in Chapter III. These differences are thought to be of little consequence, however, in comparing the derived community measure to the available national measures.

SUMMARY

In this chapter the needs for uniform sales data and constancy of input coefficients have been examined. Means of meeting these needs through industry classification and definition of sales units to be used have been outlined in some detail. The form of the table in terms of endogenous and exogenous sales and purchases has been determined. A method of determining a realized income product account from data appearing in a community interindustry table has been discussed.

In the following chapters practical ways of acquiring necessary information, the proper insertion of it into the table, manipulation of the data, and types of results to be expected will be discussed.

CHAPTER V

Data Collection

DEVELOPING AN INPUT-OUTPUT TABLE for a community, while not entirely simple, is nevertheless not an extremely complex task. The first step is selection of industry classes to be used. Rather complete discussion of this step appears in Chapter IV; the actual selection depends quite largely on the investigator's knowledge of the community to be studied. A large number of industry classes is not necessary, although each one can add to the accuracy of the analysis. Instead, emphasis must be placed upon a classification that will bring insight to proper places in the analysis.

The second step is the development of data. In taking this step, it is well to keep in mind the major areas where errors can arise and to take necessary steps to eliminate, or at least to minimize, those that can have a significant effect on the analysis. At the same time, it is important that time and means not be wasted in running down insignificant error. A number of general steps are recommended in light of these considerations.

GENERAL RECOMMENDATIONS

Accurate Totals

The first recommendation is that considerable effort be expended to obtain accurate totals for the categories being investigated. The amount of error introduced into the model by having a sizable error in one of the cells is very minor compared to the influence of even a fairly small error in one of the totals. Of course, accurate totals impose considerable reliability upon detailed estimates of transactions, since all such entries must add to the total.

Fortunately, there are many secondary sources of data that are useful in developing and/or checking totals for the various industries. Some of them are listed in the Bibliography. The use of secondary data for checking purposes, even when surveys are run, is to be encouraged. The objective is to be as accurate as possible.

Estimates of Transactions

A second major recommendation is that cells of the table be filled primarily from purchase rather than sales data. The cells are so constructed that every sale is also a purchase. In conducting surveys to obtain data, it has been noticed that purchases can be allocated among industries much more easily than sales can. In most cases it is necessary to obtain judgment data on the allocation of these factors. Businessmen need fairly detailed reports on expenditures for control and tax purposes and seem to know much more about the people from whom they buy than about the people to whom they sell. Their customers may number into the hundreds, while they may have only a half dozen or so suppliers.

Another argument in favor of the purchase approach lies in the amount of information now being made available from income tax reports by the U.S. Treasury Department. Many of the relationships shown for particular kinds of industry are applicable to local situations. Their use will contribute greatly to savings of time and effort in developing data for the table. For example, when funds and/or time are short, it may be possible to determine most of the less important relationships from these data and to concentrate more time and effort on the more important industries and on obtaining key information.

In collecting purchase data, it is especially important to obtain an accurate division of dollars spent inside the community as opposed to purchases from outside the community. In turn, less emphasis need be placed on determining accurately whether a local purchase came from local industry A or B.

Accuracy in Export Data

One of the places where considerable effort should be expended is on obtaining accurate estimates of export sales. This may mean concentrating effort on major exporting industries. Also, there are often marketing data, such as brand inspections of cattle or shipment data, that are useful in checking for major inaccuracies. Once the volume of export is determined, minor adjustments can be made in sales items in the cells that result from concentration on purchase items.

Concentration on Major Items

As was indicated previously, much more error can creep into a table from a small relative error in a major item than from a relatively large error in an unimportant item. From an efficiency standpoint, therefore, it makes sense to concentrate means and effort where the return will be greatest. It may well be that much of the opposition to the input-output approach stems from a feeling that equal accuracy must be obtained for every item in the table. The amount of accuracy required varies with survey objectives. If the objectives force concentration on certain segments of the community economy while all else becomes background, then the portion in the limelight should receive primary emphasis. In most cases these areas will coincide with major components of the economy.

THE SURVEY

Analytical studies—and many nonanalytical ones—usually depend upon the results of surveys for much of the needed information. The theory of the economic base, especially, requires knowledge of the magnitude of exchange among segments within the economy as well as between them and the outside world. In addition, there are certain segments of an economy for which no secondary data are available. Surveys are necessary in both cases.

Later in the chapter there is a discussion of major categories within a community economic system and the specific problems relating to each. First, however, a discussion of over-all survey procedure is in order.

Planning

In order to supply information needed for the table, a survey must be carefully planned. A broad classification of questions that must be considered follows:

1. *What are the purposes of the survey?*

This is extremely important. Purpose must be known before it is possible to determine items about which information is to be gathered, degree of detail, type of information, degree of accuracy, and uses to which data are to be put. At this point in the survey, therefore, it is necessary that the analyst be specific about what questions he expects to have answered. If a statistician is to be used, on a staff or on a consultant basis, he should be brought in at this point rather than later.

2. *What populations are to be surveyed?*

Generally speaking, in the analysis of a community economic system there will be six population groups that need consideration. These are (a) business and industry, (b) agriculture, (c) households, (d) local government, (e) nonlocal government, and (f) visitors. The particular analyst may want to break this down still further. Consideration of population should include, in addition to categories, types of material, geographical scope, and units about which information is desired. In general, these are determined by the purposes of the survey and by administrative and research requirements related to those purposes.

If there are marginal subgroups for which data collection is difficult, especially time-consuming, or expensive, their inclusion must be weighted against information needs. It should be kept in mind that these subgroups can be handled by special sampling procedures, if it is advisable to retain them.

3. *What information is to be collected?*

Answers to this question must stem also from purposes of the survey. Basically, the problem is to limit selection to those items that will be relevant to those purposes, that can be collected without extreme difficulty, and that will cover the field adequately. The existence of secondary data that can be used to develop certain types of information should be considered in connection with this question.

4. *How are the data to be collected?*

There are several different ways to collect data: by interviewer, mailed questionnaire, and telephone. The use of interviewers is preferred, since it allows better sampling methods, the use of special steps to cut bias, fewer refusals, and better information. It is also more costly and time-consuming, and it involves some personnel problems.

Telephone surveys are next in perference. They lack the personal touch of an interview, refusals are more frequent, and the tendency toward bias is greater. The most important recommendation for them is that they are cheaper than interviews.

Mailed questionnaires are the cheapest. They are also least desirable. The total weight of the interview must be carried by the accompanying letter. Nevertheless, they do have some advantages: (a) the respondent can answer at leisure; and (b) for certain types of questions, some personal embarrassment is avoided.

There are serious problems of nonresponse bias that must be overcome in some way. The authors consider mailed inquiries as supplements to interview surveys to cut down on costs, an excellent use.

5. *Should a form of sampling be used?*

In only a few surveys is it practical to take a complete census. Sampling, which is the selection of a part of an aggregate to represent the whole aggregate, is a long-established practice. Where the aggregate consists of similar units, as in a sack of wheat, a small sample can be taken and very little attention needs to be paid to the selection process. In the types of surveys referred to here, the aggregate will consist of many quite dissimilar units. In this case the process of sample selection is very important.

Major advantages of samples *versus* censuses are: (a) they are less difficult and costly to organize; (b) completeness and accuracy of returns are more easily ensured. By concentrating on a sample rather than on trying to take a census, more attention can be paid to accuracy of replies. Also, a sample can be more easily controlled than a census; (c) more detailed information can be obtained; (d) information is more easily handled; (e) time of field work and analysis is shortened.

(*Requirements of a good Sample.*) The principal object of a sampling procedure is to secure a sample that will reproduce as nearly as possible the characteristics of the population. People often make the mistake of trying to select "average" or "representative" units to represent a population. Such units are usually badly biased and of little actual value.

We may distinguish between two types of sampling error—those arising from bias in selection, etc., and those due to chance differences between members of the population included and those not included in the sample. The former may be termed *error due to bias;* the latter, *random sampling error.*

In addition to deliberate selection referred to above, bias may be introduced through haphazard selection processes in which some characteristic of the population becomes important, through failure to adhere to a proper random sampling process, through substitution of a convenient unit when the one selected cannot readily be found, or through failure to cover the whole of a chosen sample. If possibilities of bias exist, no fully objective conclusions can be drawn from the sample.

Once freedom from bias is assured, attention can be paid to random sampling errors. Random sampling error is approximately inversely proportional to the square root of the number of units included in the sample. Thus, the easiest way to increase the precision of a sample is to increase its size.

However, precision is related not only to the number of units but to their variability as well. There are processes of sample selection that do not introduce bias into the results, yet they reduce the part contributed by variability to sampling error. Such processes reduce the size of sample needed for a given precision. These include such restrictions as stratification, utilization of supplementary information, use of a variable sampling fraction (optimal allocation), and multistage sampling.

(The Sampling Frame.) The whole structure of a sample survey is determined by the frame. The definition of a sampling unit demands some sort of sampling frame. No detailed planning of the survey can be undertaken until the nature and accuracy of the frame are determined. If no frame exists, much of the work of the survey may be devoted to the construction of one.

Such a frame can include a list of households, a list of businesses, maps that permit sample areas to be unambiguously defined on the ground, or other similar items. Care must be taken to be sure that the information about the units listed in the frame is accurate, that there are no significant areas of omission, that there are no major duplications, that it covers all of the categories to be studied, and that it is up to date. The frame can also include an outline of proposed sampling procedure as an aid in delineating units and in getting an over-all perspective for the survey.

6. *What type of sample should be taken?*

It can be assumed that in nearly every case, surveys will be run on a sample basis. The general outline indicated above is of particular importance when procedures other than simple random sampling are used.

A random sample is the simplest type of rigorously selected sample, and it is the basis for most of the more complicated methods. The procedure, after material in the sampling frame has been designated as sampling units, is to select the required number of units.

Quite often, time, personnel, and/or monetary considerations make it impractical to select strictly random samples. In these cases it is necessary to design sampling schemes that will retain as much randomness as possible and yet will be practical for the particular project. Some of these methods will be demonstrated later in the chapter. They include the sampling processes discussed previously.

With this basic understanding of the requirements of the survey, it is now possible to examine the various categories and make recommendations for developing the information needed in each.

Business and Industry

Since business and industry provide most of the economic activity in a community, most effort will necessarily be spent with them. The categorical breakdown within this group should be made with objectives of the study and the relative importance of the various groupings in mind. Thus, study of a community dependent upon manufacturing will necessarily pay considerable attention to that industry. If needs of the analysis can best be served by setting up several classes of manufacturers, this should be done. The separation of activities of the transportation and utilities group into endogenous and exogenous functions, as discussed in Chapter III, would be another type of categorical breakdown within business and industry.

In conducting surveys to obtain information about business and industry, a number of different sampling schemes can be worked out. One that has been used successfully is a combination of stratification and ratio estimation. In applying this method, all business and industry should first be stratified into groupings as homogeneous as possible. These groupings will often be much more detailed than will be needed in the analysis and information can be collapsed before being placed in the table. As an example: If the grouping in the table is to be "all service," estimates may be prepared for lodging, personal service, business service, auto repair, other repair, hospitals, other medical services, professional service, and other services. Once estimates are prepared, they can be collapsed into the one category. The exact amount of stratification needed will depend upon the size of the community.

Listings of firms may be obtained from old age and survivors lists, files of the Bureau of Employment Security, sales tax files, business directories, and many other sources. Telephone directories are good sources also. It probably will be impossible to get a complete listing, since businesses change hands, are started, and pass out of existence so rapidly. A reasonably complete listing is desirable, however.

The next step is to determine which are the "large" firms. This must be done by setting up some sort of limit for each category beyond which firms will be considered large. In general, a firm large enough to exert considerable influence in the classification to which it is assigned should be considered large. A large service station would be considerably different from a large automobile dealer or oil refinery in any community.

At times local people may be of help in delineating large firms, but usually it is best to rely upon some sort of secondary data, such as employment, or upon the judgment of an experienced survey man. He can often classify firms by observing them for a short time.

Once the large firms are selected, all of them should be contacted for necessary information. Much of it can be furnished in response to a properly structured mail questionnaire. (See Appendix A.) All nonrespondents to a mail survey should then be contacted personally. Generally speaking, large firms recognize the fact that they can profitably utilize the information developed in a community analysis. They are, therefore, usually cooperative in furnishing information.

Once large firms have been taken care of, attention can be turned to the remainder. For some categories, the analyst may determine that he has accurate total data from secondary sources, that there are very little export sales, and that their over-all influence is going to be quite small anyway. For these he may simply determine inputs from reported data for that category as published by the U.S. Treasury Department from income tax returns. For other categories, he will want to draw a sample. In those areas where surveys have been made previously or where an area nearby has been surveyed, data will be available for use as variance components in determining sample size. At times the U.S. Bureau of the Census will determine a measure of variance from census data for a fee covering cost of such operations. Where such data are not available, samples may be drawn on a preliminary basis and size of sample determined after the survey is under way. Methods of determining adequate sample size may be found in any good sampling text.

It is suggested that the income tax format be followed as closely as possible in collecting data. An example of such an approach is to be found in the questionnaire, Appendix A. By comparing this questionnaire to the table set up for the Rawhide Community in Table VII of Chapter III, it can be easily seen that the more important items can be obtained through its use. Minor items can be allocated from secondary data found in U.S. Business Tax Returns.[1]

In the expansion of data from the sample survey, considerable improvement in accuracy can be obtained by using ratio estimation procedures. However, caution is necessary if samples are very small in particular strata, since ratio estimates become quite biased for small samples. Suitable unbiased ratio estimators have been developed, but their efficiency over simple arithmetic expansion in this case is still questionable. Where the sample is fairly large, ratio estimation is a recommended approach. The analyst should be able to find many sources of secondary data that would be useful for this purpose. Such a listing is included in the Bibliography. Most states can supply sales tax data; payroll information can be obtained from Employment Security Commissions; gasoline tax data are usually readily available.

Through the use of mailed questionnaires (as much as possible), use of data from U.S. Business Tax Returns, and the use of ratio estimation procedures, and by concentrating on items and industries of major significance, the analyst can keep the cost of obtaining needed business and industrial data within a comparable range with most other types of community analysis.

Agriculture

A great deal of information is already available on agricultural operations. The Census of Agriculture, in addition to collecting gross sales data, also collects data on payrolls and several other categories of expense. This will cover the major items in most cases. Departments of agricultural economics in agricultural colleges collect considerable cost data, but care must be used in applying them, since they often pertain to certain segments of agriculture. The U.S. Department of Agriculture has published regional data that are useful in estimating other items of cost.[2]

The extent to which purchases and sales are made outside the area of analysis can be ascertained through the use of a mailed questionnaire. Such a questionnaire can be kept rather simple, and a fairly high return can be obtained. It is not necessary to spend large sums of money to obtain information on agriculture, unless it is extremely important to the economy and detailed analysis is desired.

Household Expenditures

It is suggested that where a survey is used to obtain farm-expense data, a different group be sampled by mail to obtain household expenditure data from the agriculture segment. This will help returns on both surveys by keeping the questionnaires as simple as possible. Other types of households should be contacted personally.

Household surveys are conducted for two reasons: (1) to determine the extent of purchases of goods and services outside the area concerned, and (2) to determine the expenditure pattern of household segments. Once again, emphasis should be upon major items of expenditure. A number of sources of secondary information can be used to allocate less important items, such as the

Life Survey,[3] which gives data by regions as well as major lines; U.S. Department of Labor data on towns and regions;[4] and the U.S. Department of Commerce.[5] Emphasis in the survey can be given, therefore, to the development of purchase data that will be of most importance to the analysis.

Community directories are good sources of names for sample selection. When they are not available, geographic samples may be drawn or phone book listings used. In the latter case, those without listed phones would have no chance to be in the sample; this eliminates only a very small proportion of the population, however. Geographic samples take time and effort to design and often have larger variance than the others suggested.

We have found that samples of size 200 are adequate for determining consumption patterns of families, under most circumstances.

Government

Most data needed from government agencies pertain to local expenditures and can be obtained quite readily through a mail questionnaire. Secondary data useful for checking and for filling in the less important cells can often be obtained from published annual reports. In addition, data are available from the Census of Governments.[6] For most cities over 10,000 in population, annual data are published by the Bureau of Census.[7]

For data concerning state and federal governments there are six major categories to check: (1) payments to agriculture, (2) payments to school districts, (3) payments to welfare departments, (4) construction contracts, (5) retirement payments to individuals, and (6) employee payrolls. For local governments the most important category is payroll. Data on receipts by government from the local community are usually readily available in published reports or can be estimated from such reports.

Travelers

In areas where visitor trade is important, some means of estimating it will have to be worked out. Analysts working on a limited budget can obtain fairly good data by asking managers of lodgings, service stations, cafes, bars, and any major recreation facilities in the area what proportion of their business comes from visitors to the area. The questions can be added to the regular business survey and expanded with the other business data. An allowance should be made for purchases made from other than these categories of visitor suppliers. Another approach is to regard visitor purchases as a residual after all local and other export type purchases have been deducted from total sales by the visitor-serving categories.

In those cases where the traveler contribution is especially significant and the budget is of sufficient size, the analyst may want to conduct a more formal traveler survey. Procedures for making such a survey are covered in the handbook published recently by the Western Council for Travel Research.[8]

FILLING THE CELLS

Following the collection of necessary secondary data and the expansion of samples for the various categories, the next step is to develop estimates of sales and expenditures that will fill the various cells of the table as determined from the categories established by the analyst. Where categories have been subdivided for purposes of survey work, the subdivisions will need to be collapsed back to the major grouping.

The table itself places a fairly rigid discipline on the data. Since each cell represents both a purchase and a sale, there are aspects of double-entry accounting which place checks on each entry. Thus, the process of filling the cells will often bring errors to light that might otherwise have been overlooked.

We have found that the best initial approach is to use purchases to fill the various cells, then to check them with such sales data as are available. If surveys have been handled correctly, the estimates of purchases will fit into the table without causing much difficulty. Adjustments requiring fairly arbitrary decisions may be needed at times. If these are made within constraints imposed by total sales data and requirements of the table, they will not introduce any significant error into the analysis.

As indicated previously, there is little value in spending much time developing data for a particular cell if it is known that the relationship of the data to the over-all picture is very minor. In most cases, secondary data can be used to make these allocations without contributing any significant error. This must not be construed as an argument for using national or regional ratios to fill all the cells in a table. Communities have decided differences, but they are indicated in the major rather than the minor items in the table.

DEVELOPMENT OF MULTIPLIERS AND RATIOS

Once the input-output table is established, steps are quite clearcut. First, ratios must be established by dividing the input in each cell by total input to obtain a table of the form of Table VIII. This A matrix must then be subtracted from an identity matrix to obtain a table of the form $[I - A]$, which is then inverted to obtain a table of the form $[I - A]^{-1}$. The latter then fits into the formula derived in Chapter III, $Y = [I - A]^{-1} Z$. In most instances the researchers will need to use a computer to develop this inverse. However, in some instances a series approximation $([I - A]^{-1} = I + A + A^2 + \ldots)$, carried out for the first few terms, may be sufficient.

The inverse table is the key to understanding the community economic system, since it consists of multipliers that reflect interrelationships.

ERRORS AND THEIR EFFECTS ON THE MODEL[9]

In discussing the use of input-output models, in particular the models used herein, we are frequently confronted with the comment: "I agree completely with the conclusions drawn from your model, but I'm suspicious as to the soundness of the data contained in it. I doubt that your sampling procedure would give you figures of required accuracy." Or, in some cases: "I would like to construct a similar model, but neither our survey experience nor our project budget will enable us to collect the immense amount of data required." In answer to these comments, we submit that if proper attention is given to certain important classes of data required in constructing the model and if sound sampling techniques are used for collecting data required to supplement the vast amount of secondary data available, the task of constructing such a model of sufficient accuracy to meet most research needs becomes feasible and can even be fitted into fairly small research budgets. In support of this statement and the models used in the study, we contribute the following discussion concerning the items for which accuracy should be sought in input-output models and the methods to be used in obtaining data of the required accuracy. Of course, this discussion, as does all of this section, assumes that the theoretical requirement of constant input coefficients has been met or overcome in the applied situation.

Assume that economic activity in an economy can be summarized into only four industries: mining, utilities, trade, and household. While in reality an economy can never be quantified

TABLE XIII

INTERINDUSTRY

(IN MILLIONS OF DOLLARS)

Industry	Purchases				Export	Total Sales
	No. 1	No. 2	No. 3	No. 4		
S						
Mining (No. 1)	2	4	2	2	60	70
A						
Utilities (No. 2)	4	1	5	5	5	20
L						
Trade (No. 3)	3	2	10	25	30	70
E						
Household (No. 4)	17	8	10	0	5	40
S						
Import	44	5	43	8	0	100
Total Input	70	20	70	40	100	300

with 100 per cent accuracy, there is nothing wrong with imagining such a situation to be possible. Thus, suppose that Table XIII represents this economy's interindustry table and that no errors exist in its construction.

A table showing direct and indirect activity per dollar of export (inverse matrix) can be constructed from this interindustry table. All of the analysis could then be carried out, and forecasts of future activity could be made upon expected changes in export activity.

TABLE XIV

% ERROR IN DETERMINING PRODUCED BUSINESS
RESULTING FROM AN ERROR IN UTILITY PURCHASES
(IN MILLIONS OF DOLLARS)

Industry	Export Vector Applied	Correct Produced Output	CASE A			CASE B			CASE C		
			Purchases $	Output $	Error %	Purchases $	Output $	Error %	Purchases $	Output $	Error %
1. Mining	0	1.49	4 — 2	.88	—40.9	4 — 2	.84	—43.6	4	1.40	— 6.0
2. Utilities	5	6.01	1	5.99	— 0.3	1	5.92	— 1.5	1	5.85	— 2.7
3. Trade	0	3.12	2 + 2	3.51	+12.5	2	2.80	—10.2	2	2.43	—22.1
4. Household	0	3.21	8	3.11	— 3.1	8	2.97	— 7.5	8 — 2	2.44	—24.0
TOTALS		13.83		13.48	— 2.5		12.53	— 9.4		12.13	—12.3

For example, it may be determined from outside sources that this imaginary economy could be expected to increase its exports of utilities by five million dollars at some future time. What will the effect of this increase be on different local industries?

An answer can be obtained by multiplying the inverse matrix by the column vector (0, 5, 0, 0). While the inverse matrix is not shown here, the results of such multiplication are shown in the third column of Table XIV.

This identical use of the input-output model for this imaginary economy will now be repeated (Table XIV); however, errors will be inserted into the original 100-per-cent-accurate table at various locations. After carrying out the required manipulations, the forecasting effect of these errors can be determined by comparing their forecasted total output to that derived by use of the error-free model. Assume now that an error of two million dollars was made in the purchasing column for utilities in the interindustry table (see Case A) so that two million dollars less was shown to be purchased from mining, and two million dollars more was shown to come from trade. This error, amounting to 10 per cent of total output for utilities, of course would cause an error in the estimate of the effect on the economy from the additional five million dollars in export by utilities. By constructing a new input-output model including such an error in purchases, it was determined that the five million dollars in exports would produce $13.5 million in business and personal income or only 2.5 per cent less than was estimated by using the 100-per-cent-accurate model. These data are shown in Table XIV.

It is interesting to assume a similar-sized error in purchasing from minerals by utilities, but for contrast let us assume that this amount was then spent outside the economy instead of with the local trade industry. By building a model (Case B, Table XIV) with this error incorporated, it was determined that an error of 9.4 per cent occurred in estimating the effect of a five-million-dollar additional export by utilities.

An error of two million dollars in the payroll sector of the utility industry resulted in an over-all error amounting to 12.3 per cent for this same increase in utility exports (Case C). Data showing the individual errors occurring in the estimated effect of this five-million-dollar increase in exports are also shown in Table XIV.

From these examples it may be deduced: An error of a given magnitude, according to its location, will have quite varying effects upon an input-output model. An error that changes the leakage picture is of considerably more concern than one that results from assigning a local purchase to the wrong industry. Similarly, an error affecting household or any other industry having a high multiplier is of more concern than one affecting a sector with a low multiplier.

The above examples tend to overemphasize the effect of an error, for it is not often that only one type of export from an economy expands. To move to the opposite extreme, let us assume the forecasted increase in exports to be that all will increase by 40 per cent. The new export column vector becomes 1.5 (60, 5, 30, 5) where 1.5 is a scalar. Now, if errors occur in constructing the processing sector of the model, but both total output and exports are 100 per cent correct, the forecast will be 100 per cent correct under the conditions assumed earlier despite that error. That is:

Assume the model: $Y = Z [I - A]^{-1}$

$$Where: \quad Y = \text{correct output}$$
$$Z = \text{correct export}$$
$$[I - A]^{-1} = \text{matrix with or without an error}$$

Then: $(1.5) Y = (1.5) Z [I - A]^{-1}$

Where: 1.5   is a scalar.

It may also be shown that the condition of 100 per cent accuracy in the original export and output picture can be relaxed somewhat without application errors becoming significant, provided that the elements of the new export vector tend to be a constant proportion of the original elements (that is, if each original export can be assumed to increase by, say about 50 per cent).

CHAPTER VI

Applications

HOW TO USE THE INPUT-OUTPUT TABLE

ONCE AN INPUT-OUTPUT TABLE is prepared for a community, how can it be used? The answer to this question could make a small volume in itself. The key lies, however, in just what and how much knowledge about the local economy would be useful.

There are four tables in the analysis, and each makes a contribution to the store of knowledge. As an example: Column one can be lifted from the Monetary Transaction table (Table VII, page 31), and one can see what it will show about the Community of Rawhide. This column lists the payments made by farmers for goods and services that enter into production. Thus, farmers bought items from other farmers in the value of $3,629,000, from construction contractors in the value of $53,000, and so on down the column. The non-numbered items (nonlocal government, etc.) represent leakages from the local economy. Capital consumption (depreciation) is also considered a leakage since it goes on regardless of what happens inside the economy.

From the data presented here, it is easy to see the other industries that are influenced directly by agriculture. These will be immediately affected when farm prices fall and when they rise.

The largest contribution made by agriculture is to the household sector. This includes wages of farm workers, returns to the farmer and his family for their labor, and profits earned by the farmer as owner of the enterprise. By reference to the ratios shown for the household sector in Table VIII, page 34, the amount received from agriculture can be allocated to various segments of the economy. As would be expected, retailing receives a large share: Add together that which retailers get directly by supplying the farm business with necessary items and that received from farm households for items to maintain life and the family residence for a total of 6.5 million dollars.

83

		1-Agri	First Round Expenditures Allocation of Agricultural Payment to Household × Table VIII Ratio = Amount	
			Ratio	Amount
1.	Agriculture	3,629	-0-	$ -0-
2.	Minerals	-0-	-0-	-0-
3.	Construction	53	.0026	25
4.	Manufacturers	492	.0077	73
5.	Transportation & Utilities	1,316	.0211	199
6.	Farm Product Handlers	2,414	-0-	-0-
7.	Other Wholesalers	1,209	-0-	-0-
8.	Retailers	2,031	.4804	4,539
9.	Service	1,527	.1216	1,149
10.	Local Government	722	.0086	81
11.	Local Household	9,449	.0126	119
Leakage	Nonlocal Government	841	.1058	1,000
	Factor Earnings to Nonresidents	857	.0176	166
	Capital Consumption	3,657	-0-	-0-
	Imports	3,914	.1938	1,831
	Other	-0-	.0282	267
	TOTAL	32,111		$9,449

But this is not the whole story of the impact of the farm dollar. After each industry receives money from the farm enterprise, it pays its bills in a manner similar to that of households. Then each industry it pays does likewise, so that there is a continuous turnover of dollars. Each time, however, some part of the payment falls into the exogenous or leakage section and escapes from the economy. Thus, after a few rounds the amount left of the original farm payment becomes rather small.

To find out how much in total results from a dollar received by the farmer, turn to Table IX, page 35. This table tells what the result is after the dollars stop turning over. Now, if one desires to find out how much each industry benefited from the money paid by agriculture to the household, he can turn to the household column (page 35) and compute it; thus:

Agricultural Payment to Households

	Initial Payment	Multiplier	Induced Benefit
1. Agriculture	-0-	.0139	131
2. Minerals	-0-	.0026	25
3. Construction	-0-	.0048	45
4. Manufacturers	-0-	.0334	316
5. Transportation & Utilities	-0-	.0448	423
6. Farm Product Handlers	-0-	.0003	3
7. Other Wholesalers	-0-	.0872	824
8. Retailers	-0-	.5634	5,324
9. Service	-0-	.1593	1,505
10. Local Government	-0-	.0255	241
11. Local Household	9,449	.1722	1,627

By contrast with the column expressing just the first round of expenditures, it is seen that the farmer-household dollar actually generated $131,000 of additional local market for that industry. The minerals industry, which received nothing from the first round, ended up with $25,000 of local sales. Construction picked up an additional $20,000 through the subsequent dollar turnover, etc., again with the retailer having the largest amount. His gain from dollar turnover after the first round was an additional $785,000. Households themselves gained $1,508,000 in income.

Thus, if one adds together the amount going directly to households from agriculture ($9,449,000) to that resulting from all dollar turnover ($119,000 (first round) + $1,508,000 (subsequent rounds) = $1,627,000) he obtains total personal income of $11,076,000. This can be accomplished also by taking the multiplier from table as given, thus the original dollar paid would then be included (1.1722). This type of analysis represents one use of the input-output tables.

Referring again to Table VII (page 31) and following the row assigned to agriculture rather than the column, we get another story. Here we see the market for agricultural products. Listing the numbers in column form, we have the following:

		Sales by Agriculture
1.	Agriculture	3,629
2.	Minerals	-0-
3.	Construction Contractors	-0-
4.	Manufacturers	3,946
5.	Transportation and Utilities	-0-
6.	Farm Product Handlers	3,808
7.	Other Wholesalers	13
8.	Retailers	53
9.	Service	-0-
10.	Local Government	-0-
11.	Local Household	-0-

Exports	Sales to local investment	100
	Nonlocal Government	1,534*
	Travelers	-0-
	Other exports	19,228

TOTAL SALES $32,111

*The item of $1,534,000 attributed to nonlocal government represents, quite largely, subsidies paid by the Federal Government. Treating it the same as income from sales does no harm, and simplifies its use.

The $3,629,000 that was, previously, called a purchase by farmers from farmers, is now a sale by farmers to farmers. The input part of Table VII was considered earlier; now we shall focus upon the output part. The values in each cell in the table represent an input to the industry indicated in the column head and an output to the one listed in the row.

In the illustration here, agriculture sells heavily to manufacturing—including sugar mills, flour mills, dairies, meat packing plants, and other such processors—and to handlers of farm products—grain storage, commodity buyers and brokers, etc.—as well as to other farmers. These three, together with sales of small amounts to wholesalers and retailers, constitute the entire local market for the agricultural industry. All other sales are labeled "exports."

In the export sector are found sales of $19,228,000 to "other exports." These consist of all shipments of agricultural products made to the outside of the community being analyzed. The distance of shipment makes no difference, so long as the products go to consumers outside of the community.

Government payments are considered part of the export sector. These are actually transfer payments for which no service is performed, yet they represent new money flowing into the economy, just as do receipts from sales of products to outsiders.

The item labeled "sales to local investment" happens to be a small negative quantity in this case. This represents money reinvested in the economy by local people. However, since the model is designed to show cause-and-effect relationships, those items which do not respond immediately to forces inside the community must be handled outside the model. Investment decisions are usually long term in nature, hence are little affected by operations of one year.

We focus attention upon the export sector of the table because, in an open economy, money received for goods and services sold to "outsiders" is the lifeblood of the community. This is easily seen in a mining community, where the shipment of the mineral brings in the money to pay payrolls and taxes and to buy local supplies. When the mineral runs out, the community dies unless it can find a substitute for the basic industry.

Most communities have a diversity of basic industries, and so do not die when one industry fails, providing the others do not. Yet there are usually a few sources of basic income that are large in relation to the rest, and an understanding of the impact of each of these upon the community system is often of value.

In the Exogenous Transactions (Export) sector of Table VII, page 31, is found the following (these columns are copied as given in the table):

	Sales to Local Investment	Nonlocal Gov't.	Travelers	Others
1. Agriculture	—100	1,534	-0-	19,228
2. Minerals	-0-	-0-	-0-	28,860
3. Construction Contractors	1,627	4,783	-0-	-0-
4. Manufacturers	-0-	-0-	-0-	7,651
5. Transportation & Utilities	-0-	88	-0-	-0-
6. Farm Product Handlers	-0-	-0-	-0-	4,475
7. Other Wholesalers	-0-	-0-	-0-	354
8. Retailers	3,215	37	1,463	-0-
9. All Service	-0-	41	357	-0-
10. Local Government	-0-	2,203	-0-	-0-
11. Local Household	-0-	3,954	-0-	4,053

This segment represents the basic income of the community. Nearly everyone realizes that certain basic activities exist, but sometimes it is hard to visualize them and their relative importance to the community. The input-output table helps one to do this. But in order to get the whole story, one must also use data from two of the tables furnished by the model. The basic income data will tell only part of the story.

Now let us review the basic concepts in the community analysis. On page 8, the formula $Y = (1 — A)^{-1} Z$ was introduced; where Y is total output, $(1 — A)^{-1}$ is the community multiplier, and Z is exports. As the application of input-output was discussed, it was indicated that this model allows the development of a number of mutipliers. It is now possible to show how these multipliers help to explain how exports produce total output.

The exogenous segment copied from Table VII shows that three of the sources of basic income—Sales to Local Investment, Nonlocal Government, and Travelers—furnish money to the economy by making payments to certain industries. In order to measure the impact of each of these, it is necessary to relate each of these payments to the multipliers indicated for that industry. Such multipliers appear in the columns of Table IX, page 35. Now the reasoning behind the heading, "Direct and Indirect Activity per Dollar of Export" can be seen. Each cell value in Table IX represents the number of dollars that the industry indicated in the row will receive, through the multiplier effect, for each dollar received from outside the community by the industry indicated in the column head.

TABLE XV

DIRECT AND INDIRECT EFFECT OF EXPENDITURES BY TRAVELERS

RAWHIDE COMMUNITY

19 —

	Autonomous Original Payment (000)	Induced Income from Retail		Induced Income from Service		Total Autonomous and Induced Income (000)
		** Mult.	Income (000)	** Mult.	Income (000)	
1. Agriculture	-0-	.0247	36.14	.0040	1.43	38
2. Minerals	-0-	.0023	3.36	.0066	2.36	6
3. Construction Contractors	-0-	.0026	3.80	.0079	2.82	7
4. Manufacturers	-0-	.0540	79.00	.0185	6.60	86
5. Transportation & Utilities	-0-	.0433	63.35	.1164	41.55	105
6. Farm Product Handlers	-0-	.0016	2.34	.0001	.04	2
7. Other Wholesalers	-0-	.1783	260.85	.0823	29.38	290
8. Retailers	1,463	.1016*	148.64	.3168	113.10	1,725
9. All Service	357	.0573	83.83	.1036*	36.99	478
10. Local Government	-0-	.0171	25.02	.0765	27.31	52
11. Local Household	-0-	.2061	301.52	.5432	193.92	495
TOTAL	1,820	.5538	1,008.	.2505	456.	3,284

**Columns 8 and 9, Table IX, p. 35.

*Multiplier for induced income.

As an example, let us consider the impact of dollars spent by travelers in the Community of Rawhide (Table XV). Instead of only the original expenditure of $1,820,000, travelers were worth $3,284,000 to the community, or 1.8 times as much. Only with a very detailed analysis—such as input-output supplies—can one come to know this.

The same type of approach can be applied to the basic income resulting from expenditures by Nonlocal Government and Sales to Local Investment.

The other sources of basic income have direct multipliers appearing in the table. Notice that in calculating induced income, the numeral 1 appearing before the decimal point for the particular industry being analyzed, is dropped. This is because the

TABLE XVI

DIRECT AND INDIRECT EFFECT OF MINERAL EXPORTS ON LOCAL INCOME

RAWHIDE COMMUNITY, U.S.A.

19 —

	Autonomous Export (000)	Induced Income		Total Autonomous and Induced Income Resulting
		* Ratio	Dollars (000)	
1. Agriculture	-0-	.0012	35	35
2. Minerals	28,860	.1171	3,380	32,240
3. Construction Contractors	-0-	.0386	1,114	1,114
4. Manufacturers	-0-	.0078	225	225
5. Transportation & Utilities	-0-	.0151	436	436
6. Farm Product Handlers	-0-	-0-	-0-	-0-
7. Other Wholesalers	-0-	.0370	1,068	1,068
8. Retailers	-0-	.1412	4,075	4,075
9. All Service	-0-	.0485	1,400	1,400
10. Local Government	-0-	.0350	1,010	1,010
11. Local Household	-0-	.2916	8,416	8,416
TOTAL	28,860	.7331	21,159	50,019

*Column 2, Table IX, p. 35.

ratio includes the export dollar, and it is necessary to remove it in order to measure secondary effects.

As an illustration of the information to be gained by combining export data from Table VII, page 31, with the multipliers found in Table IX, page 35, data concerning the minerals industry have been set up in Table XVI. These data show how much benefit this particular community derived from mineral exports.

It is noticeable, for example, that for every dollar received from export, a local market was developed for this industry worth 11.7 cents. For this particular value of export, the induced local market was worth $3,380,000. Retailers were especially benefited by the turnover of these dollars, as were contractors, wholesalers, service firms, and local government.

TABLE XVII

COMPARISON OF LOCAL EXPENDITURES BY THE MINERALS INDUSTRY
WITH BUSINESS INDUCED BY MINERAL EXPORTS
RAWHIDE COMMUNITY, U.S.A.
19 —

	1 Expenditures* (000)	2 Induced Income (000)	Col. 2/Col. 1
1. Agriculture	-0-	35	Indeterminate
2. Minerals	3,443	3,380	.98
3. Construction Contractors	1,015	1,114	1.10
4. Manufacturers	-0-	225	Indeterminate
5. Transportation & Utilities	48	436	9.08
6. Farm Product Handlers	-0-	-0-	-0-
7. Other Wholesalers	472	1,068	2.26
8. Retailers	334	4,075	12.20
9. All Service	342	1,400	4.09
10. Local Government	844	1,010	1.20
11. Local Household	6,631	8,416	1.27

*Column 2, Table VII, p. 31.

Comparison of these derived data with the minerals industry expenditures shown in Table VII, page 31, can be fruitful. It can be seen at once that dollar turnover produced very little local

market for the mineral industry, aside from interindustry transfers themselves. On the other hand, retailers received almost all
of their benefit from circulation outside the mineral industry.

By now it is hoped that the reader will have gained considerable respect for the amount of information that can be obtained
from input-output tables. The illustrations cover but a few of the
possible combinations. The requirements of a particular project
and the ingenuity of the investigator are the major limits for any
one analysis.

COMMUNITY ECONOMIC SYSTEMS: WHEN AND WHY

There are numerous reasons why studies are made of community economic systems. Planning officials in particular need
detailed information. Current emphasis on economic growth
spotlights a need for Chambers of Commerce, development corporations, and others to understand the workings of the community economy. Public administrators need to know the possible effects of their decisions before they are implemented. Investors
need to know growth potential on both primary and secondary
levels before making investments.

While this book stresses the use of input-output, we recognize
that there are many other approaches that can be used. In most
applications of this model, investigators will make comple-
mentary analyses, using other tools. Deciding when to use input-
output depends upon a number of things: objectives of the study,
characteristics of the community, and research resources available. The remainder of this chapter discusses what the input-
output framework has to offer and how it will fit into general
study objectives.

Current Analysis

Often the objectives in studying a community require that as
complete a picture as possible be obtained at a particular point in
time or in a cross section of time. This requires, among other
things, that the levels of the many economic activities in the community and the many existing interrelationships be determined.
Such objectives may include inquiry into the reasons for existence
of the community or cause-and-effect relationships among the
various segments of the community.

The input-output framework is ideal for such inquiry. In its application no concern need be felt for the static nature of the framework, since the dynamics of the community over time would not be greatly involved. The rigid discipline of the framework would be especially valuable in data collection and analysis as well as in developing the needed measures of interrelationships. In utilizing an input-output model to attain objectives of this type, emphasis should first be given to the monetary transactions table (Table VII, page 31). Here, actual magnitudes of the various activities can be viewed; the market structures of each industry can be seen; and the volume and pattern of inputs can be ascertained.

The table of input coefficients (Table VIII, page 34) is produced by dividing the value of input supplied by each other industry source to a particular industry, by the total input for that industry. It extends the situation analysis in a very natural way. Input comparisons among industries can now be made directly, since the analyst is using percentages. Of course, if it were thought meaningful, a table of sales coefficients could also be developed. Such a table would have no use in the input-output model itself, but it might prove of use in making sales comparisons directly.

An example of the use of input coefficients would be a comparison of the ratios associated with households for various sectors. Another use would be a comparison of the proportion of each dollar received that remains in the community for each industry sector. The latter will explain some of the differences that occur in the next round of analysis. This round consists of the development of the direct and indirect activity table (Table IX, page 35). In order for the $[I - A]^{-1}$ matrix to have meaning it is necessary to accept the assumption of constant input coefficients, which has been discussed at length (page 22). Once this assumption is accepted, the matrix has meaning and can be used extensively in analysis.

Each element in the inverse matrix measures the amount of business received—directly and indirectly, through dollar turnover—by the industry named in the row heading from the industry or activity named in the column heading. For example, in the Rawhide Community table (IX) $1.00 in exports by manufacturers produces 15 cents in sales by retailers. Data appearing on the diagonal in the table take into account the original dollar. Thus, a dollar of exports by agriculture returns $1.19 to agriculture in Rawhide. This represents the original dollar received plus 19 cents of additional income occurring through dollar turnover in the local market. Similarly, mining exports return $1.12 to that industry for each dollar received.

Actually, each element of the inverse matrix is a special multiplier showing the relationship between a specific export and a certain industry. These multipliers may be aggregated in many useful ways. For example, it is found in the Rawhide Community that one dollar spent by an outsider in a retail store will produce $1.47 in business activity (excluding household and local government activity) and that one dollar spent with a service firm will produce $1.66 in total business activity. Now, if we refer to Table VII and select the amount spent by travelers in each kind of store, we can develop a multiplier for the traveler dollar. Thus:

$$\frac{1463}{1820} \ (1.47) + \frac{357}{1820} \ (1.66) = 1.51$$

Of course, the inverse matrix may be used in a somewhat reverse fashion to answer such questions as, "How important are various basic income sources to industry j?" This can be readily determined by multiplying the amount of basic income received through each of the major sources (Table VII) by the corresponding element in the jth industry row (Table IX). For example, in Rawhide each dollar received by farmers created 27 cents' worth of retail trade; each dollar received for mineral exports created 14 cents' worth of trade; and each dollar received for a manufactured product exported produced 15 cents for the retailer. If retailers are interested in comparing these industries on the basis of their impact upon retail stores alone, the computation is simple. Taking export values from Table VII we have the following:

Agriculture = $19,228,000 × .27 = $5,192,000 of retail trade
Minerals = 28,860,000 × .14 = 4,040,000 of retail trade
Manufacturing = 7,651,000 × .15 = 1,148,000 of retail trade

If the retailers want to see where all of their trade comes from, each of the other sources of basic income can be treated in like manner and added to these. The sum will be the total amount of retail trade in the community.

By pointing out these uses of the input-output model, it is not intended to indicate that such will constitute all of the analysis needed for a community. Depending upon the survey objectives, many other spheres of community activity may require analysis. Nevertheless, the model constitutes a rather powerful microscope for probing into the workings of a community economic system.

Measurement of Change

Quite often community researchers are especially interested in the changing complexion of the economic system. They must know where the community has been in order to forecast where it is going. Quite often, such researchers will dismiss input-output (as developed here) as of little value in such analysis because of its static nature. Instead, action is turned toward economic time series that are available for the period to be examined. This is a correct action to take. However, it must be remembered that these time series have to be related to one another and the changes within them evaluated. A reference point or base period is usually required for such comparisons. It is here that the cross-sectional analysis provided by an input-output table can be of great value.

In some instances the researchers may find the construction of an input-output model for two different periods to be worth the effort. Actually, constructing two for two different periods takes considerably less than twice the effort necessary for constructing one one-year model. As more secondary data become available, the job will become easier.

Such a two-period analysis has been conducted in two Wyoming communities. In one community, data from an earlier study were available while field data were again collected for the later year.[1] In the other community, field data were collected for one year, but secondary data were used to extend from the base to another year.[2] These two-period input-output framework comparisons proved to be extremely powerful in determining structural changes occurring in the communities studied and in pointing out the reasons for these changes.

Forecasting

An input-output model is of considerable value in forecasting expected growth in a community. In its simplest form, a new export vector is estimated for some predictive period of an available means; the forecast then results from the multiplication of that export vector by the $[I - A]^{-1}$ matrix developed for the base year.

The main advantage that the input-output model offers over more conventional techniques is that it is necessary to estimate growth in basic income only—usually a much simpler task than estimating over-all growth. Often national or large-area studies are available to help in estimating basic income. It must be stressed that the forecast of total community activity is only as reliable as the forecasts concerning basic income activities. Thus, if the objective of the community study is forecasting, at least as much investigative resources should be channeled into examining the community's export markets, their growth potential, stability, etc. as are channeled into constructing the input-output framework.

In making a forecast the researcher will also find his time well spent in determining how local industry interrelationships might change over time as well as in determining the expected future pattern of exports. Economies-of-scale, technological changes, and alterations in relative prices and trading relationships are very real forces always at work in any modern economy. Thus, a new $[I - A]^{-1}$ matrix can ideally be constructed for the economy as it is expected to be for the predictive period, before the vector multiplication is carried out. The input-output framework offers considerable advantage over other less-quantified methods in handling such structural changes by its making available for some past period a quantification of community structure.

Forecasts based on an input-output framework have a major advantage over many other techniques by reason of the detail they provide. Persons associated with individual industries can immediately see how their industry's position will change. Likewise, if unreasonableness is presented, these persons can easily point that out with the effect being a more reliable forecast. Of course, the detail required also disciplines and stimulates the researchers to avoid unreal generalizations.

Supplementing Special Purpose Studies

An input-output framework, while of considerable value in itself from a general standpoint, is also of considerable importance in relating special purpose studies to the general structure in which the particular phenomenon is located. For example, a special purpose study may be conducted regarding water availability, quality, and usage problems. It would certainly be wise to manipulate the conclusions reached in some type of general economic model, such as an input-output framework, to trace the impact of those conclusions. Structural interrelationships may very well be present that would in turn affect the basis from which the conclusions were reached.

The input-output framework is sufficiently flexible that any variables (or industries) relative to the special purpose study may be easily inserted. For example, in a water study, water usage and quality components may be inserted as industry inputs to simplify handling and determination of requirements for a certain level of output.

Advantages of Input-Output

Whenever an analysis of a community is undertaken, the researcher is soon faced with a number of questions whose answers lie in a knowledge of the cause-and-effect relationships that explain the community's existence. For this reason, the concept of the economic base has become popular. It furnishes a logical approach to questions of this nature.

In utilizing the concept, however, quite often analysis stops with a community multiplier. This measure offers some information about relationships, but it does not tell why they exist nor does it allow much detailed examination of them. Such multipliers are unstable over time and with changes in basic income patterns and do not provide a framework for the insertion of material to counterbalance these changes.

In an attempt to overcome these disadvantages of the simple community multiplier, researchers often try to upgrade the multiplier framework. For example, they will construct a separate multiplier for each of several different items of basic income. They may also hypothesize changes in these multipliers with community growth. In short, at times a great deal of effort is expended trying to improve on a basically limited tool.

It has been observed that quite often the amount of resources expended on such methods would produce a highly satisfactory input-output table. This method is, in fact, a formal extension of the community multiplier. One of its products is an over-all multiplier, but this is not regarded as one of its important contributions.

Some major advantages of this more complex analysis are:

1. It provides a framework within which basic versus non-basic activity can be identified and quantified.

2. It provides the necessary setup for tracing the impact of basic activity upon the community.

3. It quantifies local industry relationships and explains their origin.

4. It shows the relative importance of various types of economic activity. By setting up common definitions, conceptions, and terms, it allows direct comparisons to be made. Such comparisons can be made in actual values or on a ratio basis. The first emphasizes differences in industry size; the latter allows for comparison of structure without regard to size.

5. The amount of detail that can be developed allows the researcher to insert changes rather readily; thus it is possible to assess inpending change.

6. It assists forecasting by providing a framework for assessing secondary effects of forecasted developments.

7. It supplies a framework within which data for other types of analyses can be developed. For example, the need for income and product-account data can very easily be filled with the input-output framework. Once the basic relationships are determined for an input-output analysis for one year, similar tables can readily and cheaply be constructed for subsequent years. At certain intervals, depending upon the community, new surveys can be made to correct any deficiencies that arise. Even if no such surveys are made, input-output provides the best framework

for developing such accounts. After all, input-output is really just an accounting system.

8. It is the accounting concept that makes this system superior in applying discipline to the collection of data, one of its admittedly more important advantages.

It is our contention that, if a community analysis is to be attempted, beyond just superficial description, the analysts should seriously consider making use of input-output techniques. This book shows why, and will, we think, make it easier to accomplish.

CHAPTER VII

Summary

AN INCREASING INTEREST in the growth and development of communities makes it imperative that we gain greater understanding of community economic systems. This is true for activities in the United States and in the world's less developed areas. Considerable effort has been expended in trying to understand the individual consumer, the corporation, and other microunits and in gaining knowledge about the national macrostructure. The community is a collection of microunits operating within a macrostructure and might well be designated as a medioeconomic unit.

The community economic system is here defined as "a collection of activity, people, and producing units occupying a specific and recognizable geographic area, the members of which have common economic interests." This definition is intended to include the expression of the effects of social and political factors in economic terms.

The theoretical structure of such a system has been equated with the concept of an economic base. The concept requires certain basic assumptions. One of these is derived directly from the community system concept of microunits operating within a defined geographic space, each of which achieves some degree of specialization. Specialization gives rise to a need for trade. The extension of trade outside the cluster furnishes the economic base upon which the community grows in a modern economy.

A further assumption is that there is interdependence between input and output for each microunit. This interdependence is extended to assume that input equals output for each microunit. (Accumulation and depletion of inventories are not allowed in the model.) To lend still further stability, it is hypothesized that input patterns and sources of supply for any microunit are somewhat stable over time and for varying levels of output. The justification for these assumptions is given in the text. (See page 7.)

It is primarily related to the fact that economic base models are static in nature; nevertheless, they are useful in assessing the effect of change.

The economic base of a community develops from the fact that the model requires the local market to be determined by local input requirements. Thus, it cannot increase or decrease without some autonomous stimulant. Such a stimulant is provided by export activity between the community and other communities.

Let us say: $A = \dfrac{\sum_i a_1 X_1}{\sum_i X_1}$, which is the total local input coefficient; Y, total community output; X, total community input; and Z, total local exports. The relationship for the economic base is $Y = (1 - A)^{-1} Z$. The factor $(1 - A)^{-1}$ is the community multiplier. This relationship holds whether expressed in monetary or other terms.

The major difference between the community multiplier concept and domestic and foreign-trade multipliers occurs in the readjustment mechanism. The domestic multiplier, which pertains to income impact of an incremental difference between national savings and investment, and the foreign-trade multiplier, which pertains to the income impact of surpluses and deficits in foreign trade, both contain means for reaching new levels of equilibrium. Consequently, new money working its way through the economy causes the effectors to provide impulses for further growth or decline in the national economy.

In contrast, the community multiplier operates in an environment that is affected by but does not affect its source of stimulation. The community is considered insignificant in its impact on the outside world. Consequently, an injection of new money increases total activity momentarily, but as the money works its way out of the community, total activity returns to its former level. This is the factor that makes communities so sensitive to decisions that affect their basic industries.

In order for a community to thrive, it must be continually fed new money, that is, it must be able to sell its exports. When sources of new money dry up, ghost towns result. Currently, we have the example of small rural communities dying because better transportation allows farmers to trade in larger centers.

Community multipliers vary according to size, amount of industrial integration, degree of specialization of production facilities, geographic location, and aggressiveness of local businessmen. Other factors, such as resident income and consumption patterns, history of community growth, and economic maturity of the community, also have some effect.

In dynamic situations, as when a community experiences a major change in its economic base, it can be shown that the overall community multiplier is of little value. It cannot be expected to remain stable, hence is of little help in analysis. However, it can also be shown that, in such circumstances, stable relationships still exist between specific industries within the community. This is when multipliers developed through the use of input-output tables become significant.

The input-output model provides a detailed analytical framework for analysis. Whereas the over-all community multiplier approach involves aggregation of all microunits, input-output aggregates involve only those possessing similar input patterns and trade characteristics. The result is a multidimensional model, whose general form is identical to that of the community multiplier, but whose data appear in rows and columns. Instead of appearing as single numbers, total output and total exports are handled as rows in a table, each element of which represents a sale by a particular local industry to another local industry or to the outside world. Similarly, inputs are shown as columns, each element of which represents a purchase from another local industry or from the outside world.

Change is handled by the researcher's ability to define industries in such a way that the rule of constancy will hold for each one, even though it does not hold for the whole community. Input-output goes even further than this, producing submultipliers that reveal relationships among industries. This makes it possible to produce submodels that are very useful in pinpointing the effect of change.

A detailed discussion of the model, including the use of examples, is given in the text, beginning on page 21. No attempt will be made to summarize that discussion.

It is pointed out in Chapter IV that we prefer current value dollar data to other methods of delineation such as employment, measures of production, etc. The major reason for our preference is that it makes aggregation easier and makes direct comparisons among industries possible.

Problems of aggregation are the most significant ones encountered in construction of the table. The problem of constant input coefficients, which many critics of input-output stress, is closely involved. The objective of the analyst should be to plan the aggregation of microunits into industry groups, keeping in mind possible future changes, project objectives, idiosyncrasies of certain industries, and project funds. A minimal classification, set up in Chapter IV, considers three factors: (1) requirements of the economic model for validity, (2) needs of the typical user of community economic analyses, and (3) available sources of data.

Special attention is paid to the handling of dominant local industries. Disclosure problems become important in this situation, and it is necessary at times to make separate analyses that cannot be published. Some methods of collapsing these industries with others for purposes of publication are discussed.

Another problem arises from the necessity of separating the local and export markets. Since only current operational transactions among local industries are considered to be endogenous to (within) the model, purchases made by industries operating exogenously (outside the model) are eliminated in determining the local market. This part of the model is the only one that requires industry classification. All industries operating in the community, plus local government and the household sector, are to be regarded as local industries. Reasons for excluding others have their basis in the idea of response to local stimuli. If the decision to spend money in a community has little or no relation to other local activity, the industry is exogenous to the model.

For those researchers who wish to construct income and product measures similar to those published for the nation, the input-output framework offers a disciplined collection system for needed data. It is, therefore, possible to have both an income-product account and an input-output table from the same data.

Once the researcher has determined proper classification of industry, he must proceed with development of data. In doing so he should keep in mind the major areas where errors can arise and take steps to minimize those that have a significant effect on the analysis. At the same time he should be careful not to waste his resources in trying to obtain extreme accuracy in data where error has an insignificant effect.

Application of the results of input-output analysis depends upon the requirements of the analysis. There are three tables in the model, each of which contributes a great amount of information. To a certain extent the limit to use of the model is the ingenuity and imagination of the analyst.

Input-output studies will provide valuable data for many types of community activity. Planning officials are continually confronted with the need for forecasting growth. It is a great help to be able to see the secondary effects of expected changes in the basic structure of the economy. Chambers of Commerce and industrial development corporations need to understand the economic environment that they are trying to change. Public administrators also need this understanding in order to make intelligent decisions. Investors should be interested in growth potential before making investments.

In making these assertions concerning the use of the input-output framework in analyzing community economic systems, we realize that there are limitations to the method. It is not a magic "Open sesame" to complete understanding of communities. Much can be contributed by other types of models and by other disciplines, such as geography, sociology, and architecture. Our position is that the input-output framework is currently the most powerful model available to those who want to understand something of the inner workings of a community economic system.

Appendix A

ILLUSTRATIVE QUESTIONNAIRE

BUSINESS AND INDUSTRY SURVEY

1. Kind of firm ....
2. How many persons were employed here during the month of March last? ....
   A. Full-time (persons working a full work week) ....
   B. Part-time (persons working less than a full work week) ....
   C. Owners of non-incorporated businesses ....
3. What was the cost of goods sold during 19....?
   A. Merchandise $................
   B. Supplies $ ....
   C. Raw materials $................
   D. Other $................
      Total $................
4. What proportion of the cost of goods sold was purchased inside the
   ....area, from:
   A. Wholesalers   ($ or %) ....
   B. Retailers   ($ or %) ....
   C. Manufacturing   ($ or %) ....
   D. Other   ($ or %) ....
5. How much was paid during 19.... for each of the following:
   A. Salaries and wages $................
   B. Rent on business property: Local $............ Nonlocal $...........
   C. Interest on business indebtedness $................
      1. How much was interest on debt covering capital items? $..........
      2. How much was interest on noncapital items? $................
         a. What proportion of short-term debt is held by local people
            or institutions? (%) ....
   D. Taxes on business and business property:
      1. How much is property tax? $................
      2. How much is sales tax? $................
      3. Other tax $................
   E. Depreciation $................
   F. Repairs $................
      1. Building repairs ($ or %) ....
      2. Nonbuilding repairs ($ or %) ....
   G. Utilities and telephone $................
   H. Transportation $................
   I. Other $................
6. How much new construction was done in 19....? $................
7. What was the value of gross sales in 19....? $................
   A. What proportion was sold to persons living outside of the ....
      ....area ? (%) ....

105

INSTRUCTIONS TO THE INTERVIEWER

Question #1. Since the Standard Industrial Code will be used in classifying firms, you should be acquainted in a general way with the types of classification to be found there. Usually, it will be easy to identify the type of firm, i.e., grocery store, meat market, auto agency, etc. In those cases where it is not easy, fairly detailed notes will make classification easier later on.

Question #2. The month of March was chosen because most secondary data fit that month. Full-time workers are those hired employees (including managers in corporations) who are considered to be full-time in the sense of working full weeks. If a person is hired on a temporary basis but is working full weeks during March, he is a full-time employee. Part-time employees are those who work only parts of weeks.

Question #3. The concept of cost of goods sold varies with the type of firm. For retail stores and wholesale houses it would be largely merchandise, excluding transportation costs. For service firms, it could include supplies used in performing the service plus any merchandise sold, again excluding the transportation cost. For manufacturers it would be largely raw materials. If the other category covers only a minor amount, no great effort need be expended upon it. In case it covers a substantial part of the cost of goods sold, a detailed explanation will be needed. Care should be taken that no capital equipment is included in this category. Often transportation costs are included in "costs of goods sold" records; these should be ascertained and placed in 5H.

Question #4. This is a very important question. In most cases it will not add to 100, because part of the goods will be purchased outside of the area. It is necessary that the statement "purchased inside the ....area" be stressed. Most businessmen can answer these questions quite readily because they are usually concerned about purchases and have a good idea where they are made. In some cases, it may be necessary to define wholesalers, etc. When a substantial amount occurs in the "other" category, detailed explanation should be given.

Question #5. Salaries and wages—This includes all money paid out for hired help including salaries of hired managers, but excluding owners of non-incorporated businesses. *Rent*—It is important that we distinguish between rents paid to residents of the .... area and those paid to people who live outside the area. Only rent on business property should be included. *Interest*—It is necessary that interest paid on long-term debt, usually acquired in order to obtain capital items, be separated from that paid on short-term debt. It is also important that interest paid on short-term debt to local people and institutions be separated out. *Taxes*—Bases must be found for allocating tax revenues to the local government units, as well as to state and federal units. The breakdown in taxes is meant to furnish this basis. A fairly detailed discussion of the "other" category is needed where a substantial amount is recorded. *Depreciation*—This is the same depreciation item as is reported to the Internal Revenue

Service. *Repairs*—In order to properly allocate repairs, it is necessary that building repairs, which are handled by the construction industry, be separated from repairs made by repair service industries. *Utilities and Telephone*—Included here are water and sanitary services, natural gas, electricity, and telephone. *Transportation*—This includes transportation paid on goods received only. *Other*—This includes such things as bad debts, losses on business property, depletion, amortization, etc. *New Construction*—This includes everything except repairs to existing structures. *Gross Sales*—Do not include any transportation paid on products shipped out.

Notes

CHAPTER II

1. Walter Isard, *Location and Space Economy*, 2.

2. Moon H. Kang and Edgar Z. Palmer, "Multiplier Concepts," in Edgar Z. Palmer, ed., *The Community Economic Base and Multiplier*, 22.

3. U.S. Department of Commerce, Office of Business Economics, *Personal Income by States Since 1929*, 5.

4. *Ibid*. Our italics.

5. Moon H. Kang, "Multiplier of Selected Medium-Sized Communities in the Great Plains Area," in Edgar Z. Palmer, ed., *The Community Economic Base and Multiplier*, 61.

6. *Ibid*.

7. Richard E. Lund, *An Analysis of a Local Economy in a Period of Rapid Transition*, 44.

8. *Ibid*., 55. Our italics.

9. Gerald E. Thompson, "The Multiplier in Lancaster County, Nebraska," in Edgar Z. Palmer, ed., *The Community Economic Base and Multiplier*, 103-8.

CHAPTER III

1. Walter Isard, *Methods of Regional Analysis: An Introduction to Regional Science*, 338-39.

CHAPTER IV

1. Bureau of the Budget, Executive Office of the President, *Standard Industrial Classification Manual*.

2. U.S. Department of Commerce, *Personal Income by States Since 1929*, 57.

CHAPTER V

1. U.S. Treasury Department, Internal Revenue Service, *Statistics of Income—1959-60, U.S. Business Tax Returns*.

2. U.S. Department of Agriculture, Economic Research Service, *Farm Income* (a supplement to *The Farm Income Situation* for July, 1961), and U.S. Department of Agriculture, U.S. Department of Commerce, *Farmer's Expenditures in 1955 by Region*.

3. Alfred Politz Research, Inc., *Life Study of Consumer Expenditures*, Vol. I.

4. U.S. Department of Labor, Bureau of Labor Statistics, *Family Income, Expenditures, and Savings in 1950*.

5. Louis J. Paradiso and Mabel A. Smith, "Consumer Purchasing and Income Patterns," in *Survey of Current Business*, 18. U.S. Department of Commerce.

6. U.S. Department of Commerce, Bureau of the Census, *1957 Census of Governments*.

7. U.S. Department of Commerce, Bureau of the Census, *Compendium of City Government Finances*.

8. Western Council for Travel Research, Inc., *Standards for Traveler Studies* ($2.00. Copies may be purchased from Secretary-Treasurer, W.C.T.R., P. O. Box 8066, Foothill Station, Salt Lake City 8, Utah.)

9. Lund, *Analysis of a Local Economy*, 69-72.

CHAPTER VI

1. Lund, *Analysis of a Local Economy*.

2. Floyd K. Harmston, *A Study of the Resources, People, and Economy of Carbon County, Wyoming*.

Bibliography

A. BOOKS

Artle, Roland, *Studies in the Structure of the Stockholm Economy.* Stockholm, The Business Research Institute at the Stockholm School of Economics, 1959.

Barna, Tibor, ed., *Structural Interdependence and Economic Development.* London, Macmillan & Company, Ltd., 1963.

Berman, Barbara R., Benjamin Chinitz, and Edgar M. Hoover, *Projection of a Metropolis: Technical Supplement to the New York Metropolitan Region Study.* Cambridge, Mass., Harvard University Press, 1960.

Chenery, Hollis B., and Paul G. Clark, *Interindustry Economics.* New York, John Wiley and Sons, Inc., 1959.

Chenery, Hollis B., Paul G. Clark, and Vera Cao Pinna, *The Structure and Growth of the Italian Economy.* Rome, Mutual Security Agency, 1953.

Dorfman, Robert, Paul A. Samuelson, and Robert M. Solow, *Linear Programming and Economic Analysis.* New York, McGraw-Hill Book Company, Inc., 1958.

Isard, Walter, *Location and Space Economy.* New York, John Wiley and Sons, Inc., 1956.

———, *Methods of Regional Analysis: An Introduction to Regional Science.* Cambridge, Mass., The Massachusetts Institute of Technology, 1960.

Kirksey, C. D., *An Interindustry Study of the Sabine-Neches Area of Texas.* Austin, Bureau of Business Research, University of Texas, 1959.

Leontief, Wassily W., *The Structure of American Economy, 1919-1939.* Second edition. New York, Oxford University Press, 1951.

———, *Input-Output Economics.* New York, Oxford University Press, 1966.

———, and others, *Studies in the Structure of American Economy.* New York, Oxford University Press, 1953.

Rasmussen, P. Norregaard, *Studies in Intersectoral Relations.* Amsterdam, North Holland Publishing Company, 1956.

Tinberger, Jan, and Hendricus C. Box, *Mathematical Models of Economic Growth.* New York, McGraw-Hill Book Company, Inc., 1962.

Walras, Leon, *Elements of Pure Economics,* trans. by William Jaffe. Homewood, Illinois, Richard D. Irwin, Inc., 1954.

Western Council for Travel Research, *Standards for Traveler Studies.* Salt Lake City, University of Utah, 1963.

B. PAMPHLETS AND PARTS OF SERIES

Harmston, Floyd K., *A Study of the Resources, People, and Economy of Carbon County, Wyoming.* Cheyenne, Wyoming Natural Resources Board, 1962.

Lund, Richard E., *An Analysis of a Local Economy in a Period of Rapid Transition.* Laramie, University of Wyoming, 1962.

Martin, William E., and Harold O. Carter, *A California Interindustry Analysis Emphasizing Agriculture.* Part I. Giannini Foundation Research Report No. 250. Division of Agricultural Sciences, University of California. Davis, 1962.

Politz, Alfred, Research, Inc., *Life Study of Consumer Expenditures.* New York, Time, Inc., 1957.

Tiebout, Charles M., *The Community Economic Base Study.* Supplementary Paper No. 16. New York, Committee for Economic Development, 1962.

C. GOVERNMENT PUBLICATIONS

U.S. Department of Agriculture, *Agriculture Statistics.* Washington, Government Printing Office. Annual.

U.S. Department of Agriculture, *Farm Employment by States.* Washington, Government Printing Office, 1958. Statistical Bulletin #236.

U.S. Department of Agriculture, *Major Statistical Series,* Vol. 1-9. Washington, Government Printing Office, 1957. Agriculture Handbook #118.

U.S. Department of Agriculture, Agricultural Research Service, *Farm Costs and Returns Series.* Washington, Government Printing Office. Annual.

U.S. Department of Agriculture, Bureau of Agricultural Economics, *Meat Animals, Farm Production, Disposition, and Income by States.* Washington, Government Printing Office, 1952. Statistical Bulletin #113.

U.S. Department of Agriculture, Bureau of Agricultural Economics, *Meat Animals, Farm Production, Disposition, and Income by States.* Washington, Government Printing Office, 1956. Statistical Bulletin #184, 1950-1954, Revised Estimates.

U.S. Department of Agriculture, Economic Research Service, *Farm Income.* Washington, U.S. Department of Agriculture, August, 1961. A supplement of the *Farm Income Situation* for July, 1961.

U.S. Department of Agriculture, U.S. Department of Commerce, *Farmer's Expenditures in 1955 by Region.* Washington, Government Printing Office, April, 1958. Statistical Bulletin #224.

U.S. Department of Commerce, Bureau of the Census, *1957 Census of Government.* Washington, Government Printing Office, 1959.

U.S. Department of Commerce, Bureau of the Census, *Compendium of City Government Finances.* Washington, Government Printing Office. Annual.

U.S. Department of Commerce, Office of Business Economics, *Personal Income by States Since 1929.* Washington, Government Printing Office, 1957. A supplement to the *Survey of Current Business.*

U.S. Department of Labor, Bureau of Labor Statistics, *Family Income, Expenditures, and Savings in 1950.* Washington, Government Printing Office, June, 1953. Bulletin #1097, revised.

D. PERIODICALS

Ara, Kenjiro, "The Aggregation Problem in Input-Output Analysis," *Econometrica,* 27:257-62 (April, 1959).

Arrow, Kenneth J., and Gerard Debreu, "Existence of an Equilibrium for a Competitive Economy," *Econometrica,* 22:265-90 (July, 1954).

Briggs, F. E. A., "On Problems of Estimation in Leontief Models," *Econometrica,* 25:444-55 (July, 1957).

Buchanan, Norman S., "Deliberate Industrialization for Higher Incomes," *The Economic Journal,* 56:633-53 (December, 1946).

Bureau of Business and Economic Research, University of Maryland, College Park, "A Regional Interindustry Study of Maryland," *Studies in Business and Economics*, 8:2 (September, 1954), p. 12.

Bureau of Business and Economic Research, University of Maryland, College Park, "Estimating Maryland Government and Business Potentials," *Studies in Business and Economics*, 8:4 (March, 1955), p. 15.

Cameron, Burges, "The Construction of the Leontief System," *The Review of Economic Studies*, 19:19-27, 1950-51.

———, "New Aspects of Australia's Industrial Structure," *Economic Record* 34:362-74 (December, 1958).

Carden, John G. D., "Input-Output Analysis for Mississippi," *Mississippi's Business*, 20:1-7 (February, 1962).

Chipman, John S., "The Multi-Sector Multiplier," *Econometrica*, 18:355-74 (October, 1950).

———, "Professor Goodwin's Matrix Multiplier," *The Economic Journal*, 60:753-63 (December, 1950).

———, "A Note on Stability, Workability, and Duality in Linear Economic Models," *Metroeconomica*, 6:1-10 (April, 1954).

Dorfman, Robert, "The Nature and Significance of Input-Output," *The Review of Economics and Statistics*, 36:121-33 (May, 1954).

Evans, W. Duane, and Marvin Hoffenberg, "The Interindustry Relations Study for 1947," *The Review of Economics and Statistics*, 34:97-142 (May, 1952).

Fei, John Ching-Han, "A Fundamental Theorem for the Aggregation Problem of Input-Output Analysis," *Econometrica*, 24:400-412 (October, 1956).

Fisher, Walter D., "Criteria for Aggregation in Input-Output Analysis," *The Review of Economics and Statistics*, 40:250-60 (August, 1958).

Fouraker, Lawrence E., "A Note on Regional Multipliers," *Papers and Proceedings of the Regional Science Association*, 1:H-1—H-8, 1955.

Frisch, Ragnar, "On the Notion of Equilibrium and Disequilibrium," *The Review of Economic Studies*, 3:100-105 (February, 1936).

Georgescu-Roegen, N., "Fixed Coefficients of Production and the Marginal Productivity Theory," *The Review of Economic Studies*, 3:40-49 (October, 1935).

Grunfeld, Yehuda, and Zvi Griliches, "Is Aggregation Necessarily Bad?" *The Review of Economics and Statistics*, 42:1-13 (February, 1960).

Hagger, A., "Matrix-Multiplier Analysis: An Exposition," *Yorkshire Bulletin*, 10:19-34 (June, 1958).

Hansen, W. Lee, and Charles M. Tiebout, "An Intersectoral Flows Analysis of the California Economy," *The Review of Economics and Statistics*, 55:409-18 (November, 1963).

Hartland, Penelope, "Inter-Regional Payments Compared With Inter-National Payments," *The Quarterly Journal of Economics*, 63:392-407 (August, 1949).

Hawkins, David, and Herbert A. Simon, "Some Conditions of Macro-Economic Stability," *Econometrica*, 17:245-48 (July-October, 1949).

Heady, Earl O., and John A. Schnittker, "Application of Input-Output Models to Agriculture," *Journal of Farm Economics*, 39:745-58 (August, 1957).

Hirsch, Werner Z., "Inter-Industry Relations of a Metropolitan Area," *The Review of Economics and Statistics*, 41:360-69 (November, 1959).

——, "An Application of Area Input-Output Analysis," *Papers and Proceedings: Regional Science Association*, 5:79-92, 1959.

Hoch, Irving, "A Comparison of Alternative Interindustry Forecasts for the Chicago Region," *Papers and Proceedings: Regional Science Association*, 5:217-35, 1959.

Hurwicz, Leonid, "Input-Output and Economic Structure: A Review Article," *The American Economic Review*, 45:626-36 (September, 1955).

Isard, Walter, "The General Theory of Location and Space-Economy," *The Quarterly Journal of Economics*, 63:476-506 (November, 1949).

——, "Interregional and Regional Input-Output Analysis: A Model of a Space Economy," *The Review of Economics and Statistics*, 33:318-28 (November, 1951).

——, and Robert E. Kuenne, "The Impact of Steel Upon the Greater New York-Philadelphia Industrial Region," *The Review of Economics and Statistics*, 35:289-301 (November, 1953).

Kavesh, Robert A., and James B. Jones, "Differential Regional Impacts of Federal Expenditures," *Papers and Proceedings of the Regional Science Association*, 2:152-67, 1956.

Klein, L. R., "On the Interpretation of Professor Leontief's System," *Review of Economic Studies*, 20:131-36, 1953.

Leven, Charles L., "Measuring the Economic Base," *Papers and Proceedings of the Regional Science Association*, 2:250-58, 1956.

Machlup, Fritz, "Period Analysis and Multiplier Theory," *Quarterly Journal of Economics*, 54:1-27, 1939.

Miller, Ronald E., "The Impact of the Aluminum Industry on the Pacific Northwest: A Regional Input-Output Analysis," *The Review of Economics and Statistics*, 29:200-209 (May, 1957).

Moore, Frederick T., and James W. Peterson, "Regional Analysis: An Interindustry Model of Utah," *The Review of Economics and Statistics*, 37:368-81 (November, 1955).

Moses, L. N., "A General Equilibrium Model of Production, Inter-regional Trade and Location of Industry," *The Review of Economics and Statistics*, 42:373-97 (November, 1960).

——, "Location Theory, Input-Output, and Economic Development: An Appraisal," *The Review of Economics and Statistics*, 37:308-14 (August, 1955).

McManus, M., "Self-Contradiction in Leontief's Dynamic Model," *Yorkshire Bulletin*, 9:1-21 (May, 1957).

——, "General Consistent Aggregation in Leontief Models," *Yorkshire Bulletin*, 8:28-48 (June, 1956).

Paradiso, Louis J., and Mabel A. Smith, "Consumer Purchasing and Income Pattern," *Survey of Current Business*. Washington, Government Printing Office (March, 1959).

Ram, Peretz, "An Input-Output Analysis of a Small Homogeneous Agricultural Area," *Journal of Farm Economics*, 40:1909-20 (December, 1958).

Roosa, Robert V., "A Multiplier Analysis of Armament Expenditure," *The American Economic Review*, 31:249-65 (June, 1941).

Rosenblatt, David, "On Linear Models and the Graphs of Minkowski-Leontief Matrices," *Econometrica*, 25:325-38 (April, 1957).

Sirkin, Gerald, "The Theory of the Regional Economic Base," *The Review of Economics and Statistics*, 41:426-29 (November, 1959).

Theil, H., "Linear Aggregation in Input-Output Analysis," *Econometrica*, 25:111-22 (January, 1957).

Tiebout, Charles M., "Regional and Interregional Input-Output: An Appraisal," *Southern Economic Journal*, 24:140-47 (October, 1957).

Wolfe, Martin, "The Concept of Economic Sectors," *The Quarterly Journal of Economics*, 69:402-20 (August, 1955).

E. UNPUBLISHED MATERIALS

Carden, John G. D., and F. B. Whittington, Jr., "Input-Output Analysis of Mississippi," Mimeographed paper delivered before the Regional Science Association, Western Section, Eugene, Oregon, June 15, 1963.

Kavesh, Robert Allyn, "Interdependence and the Metropolitan Region: An Extension of Input-Output Analysis," Ph.D. dissertation, Harvard University, May, 1953.

F. ESSAYS AND ARTICLES IN COLLECTIONS

Christ, Carl F., "A Review of Input-Output Analysis," in Raymond W. Goldsmith, ed, *Input-Output Analysis: An Appraisal*. National Bureau of Economic Research. Princeton, Princeton University Press, 1955, 137-82.

Hirsch, Werner Z., "Application of Input-Output Techniques to Urban Areas," in Tibor Barna, ed., *Structural Interdependence and Economic Development*. Geneva, St. Martin's Press, 1963, 151-68.

Kang, Moon H., and Edgar Z. Palmer, "Multiplier Concepts," in Edgar Z. Palmer, ed., *The Community Economic Base and Multiplier*. Lincoln, University of Nebraska Press, 1958, 10-40.

Leontief, Wassily, "The Input-Output Approach in Economic Analysis," in H. E. Stenfert Kroese, ed., *Input-Output Relations: Proceedings of a Conference on Interindustry Relations Held at Driebergen, Holland*. Leiden, The Netherlands Economic Institute, 1953, 1-30.

Marishima, Michio, "A Reconsideration of the Walras-Cassel-Leontief Model of General Equilibrium," in Kenneth J. Arrow, Samuel Karlin, and Patrick Suppes, eds., *Mathematical Methods in the Social Sciences*. Stanford, Stanford University Press, 1960, 63-76.

Markowitz, Harry, "Industry-wide, Multi-industry and Economy-wide Process Analysis," in T. Barna, ed., *The Structural Interdependence of the Economy*. Proceedings of a Conference at Varenna in 1954. New York, John Wiley and Sons, Inc., 1956, 121-50.

Sevaldson, Per, "Change in Input-Output Coefficients," in Tibor Barna, ed., *Structural Interdependence and Economic Development*. Geneva, St. Martin's Press, 1963, 308-28.

Ullman, Edward L., "The Basic-Service Ratio and the Areal Support of Cities." Address delivered before the Association of Pacific Coast Geographers, Santa Barbara, California, June 8, 1953. Quoted in Edgar Z. Palmer, ed., *The Community Economic Base and Multiplier*. Lincoln, University of Nebraska Press, 1958.

G. SOURCES OF SECONDARY DATA FOR CHAPTER V

U.S. Department of Agriculture, Farm Income Situation; Quarterly; Washington, U.S. Department of Agriculture, Economic Research Service.
Data on gross agricultural income by state, by major source, annually.

U.S. Bureau of the Census, *U.S. Census of Agriculture*: 1959. Vol. I, Counties, Part 40, *(STATE)*; Washington, Government Printing Office, 1961.
This publication is issued every five years by state and counties. Data on gross agricultural income by state and county by major source, every five years. Also includes some expenditure data.

U.S. Bureau of Mines, Regional Divisions of Mineral Resources, *Minerals Yearbook*. Washington, Government Printing Office.
This publication is issued annually, and the number of volumes will vary. Data on value of minerals produced by kinds of mineral, states, and, in some years, counties, given annually but is usually several years behind.

U.S. Department of the Interior, Bureau of Mines, *Mineral Production in (STATE) in (YEAR)*, Preliminary Annual Figures: Region *(NUMBER)*.
Division of Mineral Resources in Cooperation with the Geological Survey of *(STATE)*, mimeographed in January of each year.
Current data on mineral production by states. See also state minerals departments and state taxing agencies for supplementary data.

F. W. Dodge Corporation, *Construction Contracts*, Summary: *Region (NUMBER)*. Monthly; New York, McGraw-Hill, Inc.
Data on construction are available on a limited basis only. Data based on building permits plus some survey materials are included in this reference.

U.S. Department of Commerce, Business and Defense Services Administration, *Construction Review*. Monthly; Washington, Government Printing Office.
These data are based on building permits only with no adjustments such as those in the Dodge data. This is a partial census, but is not a sample.

U.S. Bureau of the Census, *U.S. Census of Manufacturers*: 1958. Area Report MC58 (3)-49, *(STATE)*; Washington, Government Printing Office, 1961.
Data on manufacturing plant numbers, payrolls, value added, and annual investment. Occasionally data on value of gross product, by state, county, and city. Published approximately every five years.

U.S. Bureau of the Census, *Annual Survey of Manufacturers*: 1957. Washington, Government Printing Office, 1959.
Data on numbers of firms and value added. Released only for certain years.

U.S. Bureau of the Census, *U.S. Census of Business*: 1958. Wholesale Trade, Area Bulletin W-1-50 *(STATE)*; Washington, Government Printing Office, *(DATE)*.
Data on numbers, payroll, gross business for all wholesalers, and gross sales by merchant wholesalers and others. State, county, and city data. Published approximately every five years. Other sources include state taxing agencies.

U.S. Bureau of the Census, *U.S. Census of Business: 1958*. Retail Trade, BC58-RA50, *(STATE)*; Washington, Government Printing Office, *(DATE)*, 1960.

Data on retail sales by selected categories, and total retailer numbers and payroll for all retailers. Published approximately every five years. Other sources of information on retail sales include sales and use tax plus other taxing agencies.

U.S. Bureau of the Census, *U.S. Census of Business: 1958*. Selected Services, BC58-SA50, *(STATE)*; Washington, Government Printing Office, 1960.

Data on selected services, with some breakdown by type, state, county, and city data. Released about every five years. Does not include data on medical health services, professional services, or nonprofit institution services.

U.S. Treasury Department, Internal Revenue Service, *Statistics of Income-1959-60. U.S. Business Tax Returns* (Publication No. 438-8-62); Washington, Government Printing Office, 1962.

Some data on services on a national basis. Fairly detailed breakdown.

U.S. Department of Commerce, Office of Business Economics, *Survey of Current Business*. All August issues; Washington, Government Printing Office *(YEAR)*.

U.S. Department of Commerce has also issued a supplement to the Survey of Current Business, *Personal Income by States Since 1929*. Data are available by states on personal income categorized by major sources. Available 1929 to date. In many states a state agency will prepare county data comparable to this.

U.S. Bureau of the Census, *Statistical Abstract of the United States: 1962*. Eighty-Third Edition; Washington, Government Printing Office, 1962.

Government revenues are available from several sources. Local units quite often publish statements of revenue and disbursements. Care must be taken to identify all special districts which carry on government functions. Nonlocal revenues are also a matter of public record, but not all states have good reports. This reference reports on state as well as federal expenditures. Federal tax collected by state is an important item.

Index

Accuracy: of data in cells, 67; sought for, 79; relaxation of condition, 82

Aggregate of dollars: used to represent total output, 19

Aggregation: determination of classes, 23; comparison of input-output with usual approach, 23; and the rule of constancy, 24; controlled by objectives of study, 43; of activity has bearing on constant coefficients, 43; activities into industries, 43; of industries when change is correlated, 43; based on simplicity of adjustments, 44; basic minimum, 44; affected by available funds, 44; and objectives of study, 44; and importance of industry, 44; by major activity, 45; problems, 103. *See also* Agriculture; Mining; Manufacturing; Retailing; Services; Wholesaling

Agriculture: effect on multipliers, 17; distinctness of, as a sector, 45; delineation of type depends on objectives of survey, 46; sources of data concerning, 75

Amortization: of investment in mining, 46

Application of input-output: dependence on requirements of analysis, 104

Autonomous stimulant: needed for expansion or contraction, 101. *See also* Basic income

Availability of data: in delineation and selection of measurement units, 42

Availability of funds: effect on aggregation, 44

Availability of resources: and changing input patterns, 7

Barriers to trade: influence on multiplier, 17

Basic activities: assignment of jobs to, 10; input-output as aid in visualizing, 88

Basic income: related to exports, 9; cause of temporary increase in activity, 12; related to specific industries versus aggregates, 19; impact of large sources, 82; forecasts concerning, 96. *See also* Economic base

Basic industries: difficulties of definition, 26; diversity as hedge for community, 87

Bias: introduction of, 71

Building construction: as part of construction sector, 47

Business and industry: s a m p l i n g schemes for, 72

Businessmen: as sources of traveler expenditures, 76

Capital consumption: as an exogenous input, 60. *See also* Depletion allowances

Capital expenditures: short-term possibly endogenous, 58. *See also* Investment

Capital investment: an exogenous factor, 48; relation to construction, 48. *See also* Investment

Casualness: methods of overcoming, 13. *See also* Community multiplier

Categories: related to government, 76

Cause and effect: revealed by input-output, 92

Cells of table: information to be comparable, 48; purchases and sales represented, 77. *See also* Transactions table

Change: stimulus from outside community, 14; handled by aggregation, 24; occurring in industry components, 43; reason for analysis, 43; as a factor in delineation, 46; handling of, by analyst, 102

Changes in inventory: part of agriculture's sales, 45

Characteristics of community: a determinant for use of input-output, 92

Churches: inclusion with household, 53

117

activity, 33; of transportation, 49; use of, 93. *See also* Constant input coefficient

Input-output methods: differences in, 21; application to community system, 21, 97; and outside trade, 23; analytical framework, 23, 33, 92, 95, 104; format for data collection, 27; for different time periods, 95; flexibility, 97; advantages of, 98-99, 102, 104; limitations, 104

Instability: and the economic system, 5; of coefficients, 8, 38, 42, 44, 100

Interdependence: between input and output, 6, 100; through basic income linkages, 14

Interest: in community systems, 1

Interindustry transactions: of local government units, 54. *See also* Transactions table

Interviewers: use of, in surveys, 69

Inventories: accumulation and depletion not allowed, 7, 100; agricultural, 58-59

Inverse matrix: contrast with community multiplier, 13, 23, 26, 98; significance of, 26; formation of, 28-29; use of, 78, 93-95. *See also* Multipliers

Investment: treated exogenously, 13, 87; decisions concerning, 30; mining services as, 47

Irrigation: in agricultural aggregation, 46

Job: definitional problems, 10

Labor officials: and community analysis, 2

Large firms: sample of, 73; cooperation of, 74. *See also* Dominant industries

Large sample: relation to ratio estimation, 74

Leakage: relationship to error, 82. *See also* Import row

Life survey of family expenditures: as a source of data, 76. *See also* Household

Linear homogeneous function: requirement, 36

Lists: as sampling frames, 71-73

Local activity: determinant of transactions level, 32. *See also* Endogenous transactions

Local final demand: both exogenous and endogenous, 30

Local government: definition, 53; as an industry, 56; treated endogenously, 57

Local highway construction: treated exogenously, 32. *See also* Capital investment

Local industry: delineation of, in model, 42; defined, 56-57. *See also* Endogenous transactions

Local market: affected by impending change, 2; local input patterns, 8; separation from export, 103. *See also* Community economic systems

Local savings: impact on growth, 13. *See also* Leakage

Lower limits: significance of, 41

Macroeconomic system: concentration on, 1, 2; defined, 5. *See also* National economies

Magnitudes: viewed in transaction table, 93

Mailed questionnaires: use of, in surveys, 70

Major activity: guide to aggregation, 45

Major items: influence of error in, 68. *See also* Errors

Manipulative model: changes needed in base, 40

Manufacturing: aggregation, 48; value of sales, 50; as dominant industry, 55

Maps: as sampling frames, 71

Marginal subgroups: inclusion of, 69

Market value: as unit of measurement, 22. *See also* Dollar sales

Measurement: preferred units of, 26; change reflected in two models, 95

Medical services: data not collected, 53

Medioeconomic system: defined, 5, 100

Medium of exchange: use of, to equate imports and exports, 9

About the Authors

FLOYD K. HARMSTON has been Professor of Economics since June, 1966, and Assistant Director for Business and Economic Research in the Research Center of the School of Business and Public Administration of the University of Missouri at Columbia since September, 1965. During the previous ten years he was Director of the Division of Business and Economic Research in the College of Commerce and Industry of the University of Wyoming at Laramie.

Dr. Harmston has received degrees from Utah State University (B.S. in Commerce, 1940); the University of Wyoming (M.S. in Statistics, 1955); and the University of Missouri (Ph.D. in Economics, 1966). He is author or coauthor of twelve monographs that are analyses of community economies prepared for and published by the Wyoming Natural Resources Board. Dr. Harmston's findings concerning techniques of analyzing functional and governmental segments of the economy have been published in the professional journals and as publications of local governments and federal agencies. He has also prepared input-output models of the Missouri economy that are being published as part of the Missouri Economy Series of the Business and Public Administration Research Center.

• • •

RICHARD E. LUND is research associate in the Statistical Laboratory at Iowa State University, Ames. He has earned degrees at the University of Omaha (B.A., 1957) and at the University of Wyoming, Laramie (M.S. in Industrial Management, 1960; M.S. in Statistics, 1962).

Mr. Lund's analyses of local economies have been published variously as articles in professional journals and as reports by the Small Business Administration of the federal government, the University of Wyoming, and the Wyoming Natural Resources Board.